ACHIEVING PEACE OF HEART

ACHIEVING PEACE OF HEART

by

NARCISO IRALA, S.J.

Missionary,
China and Formosa

TRANSLATED BY

LEWIS DELMAGE, S.J.
Saint Joseph's College
Philadelphia, Pa.

Over 100,000 copies in print
This printing October, 1966

NEW YORK CITY

JOSEPH F. WAGNER, INC.
HERDER, LONDON

Imprimi Potest:

JOHN M. DALEY, S.J.
    Praep. Prov. Marylandiae

WASHINGTON, D.C., MAY 31, 1963

Nihil Obstat:

JOSEPH A. M. QUIGLEY
    Censor Librorum

Imprimatur:

✠ JOHN J. KROL, D.D., J.C.D.
    Archbishop of Philadelphia

PHILADELPHIA, SEPTEMBER 13, 1963

1964 REVISED AND ENLARGED EDITION

Translator's Introduction
to the Revised Edition

THE "GLACIER-PRIEST," Father Bernard Hubbard, S.J., made the missions in Alaska known to hundreds of thousands of Americans by his slide lectures and color movies of mission life in Alaska. Years ago Father Irala began, as a kind of counterpart of Father Hubbard, lecturing in the Americas about the missions in China. He had had many years of experience in China, and later in Formosa, and so could portray factually and graphically many sides of mission activity. He travelled all over the United States and throughout Latin America as well. But Father Irala found that many people in our time felt a great need to solve personal problems. Indeed, these personal problems obscured their vision of larger human efforts both here at home and in fields afar. They would come in droves to hear about the workings of the human heart and emotions, how to use their minds more effectively, or about the daring pursuit of a noble ideal. They wanted to lead better lives and work for a better world. They were no longer so interested in seeing pictures of foreign lands or hearing about strange customs. "Here is a better approach," he said. "I will try to help people put to better use the great powers God has given them, their minds and hearts, their emotions and feelings, their enthusiasm. Then they will be better able to come in close contact with beauty and truth, goodness and grace. And so I may help open their minds and hearts to the great vision of humanity and of the work of Christ's Church."

Father Irala soon found he had to devote all his time and energy to these lectures and to personal consultations. Some personal problems, of course, needed specialized assistance. So they were referred to the proper clinics or doctors for diagnosis and therapy. But thousands of other problems were not in a category which demanded psychiatric assistance. Indeed, every teacher, doctor, parent, priest or guidance counsellor is regularly called upon to help with such problems.

Soon other priests, educators and doctors demanded that he give his lectures a more permanent form by publishing them. He did so, and subsequent experience and consultations have resulted in revisions and additions to his book through twenty-seven editions. These changes are included in this English edition. The chapter, "How to Rest" has been enlarged because of the enormous need of it; so many people are ignorant even of how to sleep right. And need has dictated the inclusion of a section on avoiding voice fatigue. The chapter, "How to Think" has been dropped because it has been developed into a separate volume entitled *Mental Efficiency without Fatigue* (Joseph F. Wagner, Inc., 53 Park Place, New York 7, N. Y.). Acknowledgment is due and is hereby gratefully expressed to Miss Mary Jane Lyons for her painstaking care in the preparation of the manuscript for this edition.

LEWIS DELMAGE, S.J.

Philadelphia, Pa., 1963

Translator's Introduction
to the First Edition

FATHER IRALA'S ORIGINAL WORK, *O Contrôle Cerebral*, was first published at S. Paõlo, Brazil, in 1944. Shortly thereafter various foreign language translations appeared in Europe and Latin America and were as enthusiastically received as the original Portuguese edition. But until now the work was unavailable to English-speaking readers—an omission which the present authorized translation has finally remedied.

The need for such a book is readily apparent. All of us at one time or another experience what—in the jargon of the psychologist—are called "personality maladjustments." These may be and usually are minor mental disturbances of one kind or another—doubt, worry, fear, and so forth—which, while not always requiring the specialized (and expensive) services of a psychiatrist, need very much to be corrected and avoided. To this end we need a practical handbook or manual that will outline an effective method of procedure. This translation of Father Irala's work does, we feel, more than adequately fulfill that need.

However, a word of warning may not be out of place at this point. Father Irala never intended this book as a panacea for all mental ills of whatever kind or degree. He does not pretend that the serious complications of a neurosis or psychosis admit of any facile solution to be found in the pages of this or any other manual. Special disorders must continue to require the attention of the specialist. But the ordinary, everyday problems of inefficiency, mental wandering, worry, overwork, insomnia, and loss of self-control, these he feels may be treated and an effective cure found for them in the manner here indicated.

The important thing is that Father Irala's methods have been found to work. His book is a manual of practice. It is meant, as the author himself says, not to be read on the run but to be studied and put into practice. Professional men who have read the manuscript—educators, guidance counsellors, and directors of souls—have already testified to its effectiveness. But even more impressive has been the testimony of those who have personally profited from the author's work. Many of these actual cases are detailed throughout the text; many more have been by word of mouth; many, finally, have come to the author in a steady stream of letters and correspondence from all over the world. People who have never met him but who have read his book in Spanish, Portuguese, Italian, or Polish, have written to ask his advice or to tell him how much he has helped them.

The author is, of course, a Catholic priest. His book is the product of years of experience both as a priest and as a practicing psychologist. It is a book, therefore, written out of knowledge and charity, and as such it will prove equally valuable to all—regardless of religious belief—who take it up in an awareness of their own need and with a true desire for self-help. For surely they are not only Catholics who experience bouts of depression; the experience is universal and has universal implications. All man's dreams and daring, all the richness of his emotional and affective life, all this forms a unity with his rational activity. Intellect and will are not discarnate. The whole man acts, thinks, desires, loves, hopes and fears. All this human activity has been symbolized by the human heart—for, indeed, do we not say that a man is great-hearted, hard-hearted, chicken-hearted, weak-hearted? And for those who do believe, all man's ideals are symbolized and incarnate in the Heart of Christ. The peace of that Heart, which He would give to us, is there to be had, to be achieved. Father Irala outlines for us how many natural means, too, can help us to that supernatural goal.

Grateful acknowledgment is here made to the Rev. Charles J. Lewis, S.J., for his careful reading and checking of the entire manuscript, and to the Rev. Mark H. Bauer, S.J., for his advice on the use of biological and medical terms.

L. D.

To
all who would direct
their feet in the way of peace of heart—

THIS BOOK IS

EARNESTLY DEDICATED

Preface

THE DANGERS of the atomic age in which we live are outward signs of a still more terrible, because interior, explosive force. The mental life of modern man, his thoughts and impulses, his desires and feelings, his nervous breakdowns and chaotic hurrying and worrying, all these are more immediately threatening than atomic warfare.

Almost every month we discover new scientific, industrial, and political frontiers. We live in a day of atomic reasearch, atomic explosions, atomic history. All the day long we are exposed to explosive impressions from newspapers, radio, TV and the movies; in travel we ride the protracted explosion of jet planes; and we frequently find our business and social life building up frantically to an explosive potential. Everywhere we seem to have a thousand harrying details to attend to, and we find it harder and harder to live within the framework of twenty-four hours. All this exerts a fearful pressure on our interior life, so great a pressure indeed that to many of us our personal lives seem little more than one minor explosion after another.

Such is the experience, even in the most technologically advanced nations, of men of the highest ideals who have the best intellectual and managerial talent. American statistical sources speak of 19,000,-000 persons needing sleeping pills every night.

These are among the 10 million diagnosed as neurotics and another 20 million without that official
predicate. So many executives in business and indus-
try have developed gastric or duodenal ulcers that
this disease has been classified as an occupational
hazard for them. There is so much hypertension and
so many coronary illnesses among business executives
that they are said to account for half of the total
number of such cases.

In our thinking we no longer have that Socratic
calm in which ideas follow one another in order.
We have exchanged the Greek "sophrosyne," or clas-
sic poise, for a ragged horde of images and ideas.
We lack the peace we need to concentrate our attention on one individual idea. From this come confusion, mental fatigue, nervousness, uneasiness,
insomnia, and the like.

In our feelings that moderation of our forefathers,
as well as the healthy and holy gaiety of their family life, is yielding place to abnormal or incoherent
impressions, precocious or even brutal impulses, and
exaggerated fears or desires. These become in-
grained or magnified, or transfer themselves to
undue objects. They give rise to all kinds of unreasonable fears (phobias), obsessions, anxieties,
worries and troubles.

In our decisions and goals we are no longer per-
sonalities with fixed norms to follow. Nor do we
face the problems of life courageously and overcome its difficulties. On the contrary we find people
without principles or strength of will, men and sometimes youths who are so disillusioned that they will
even go to the extreme of committing suicide. They
have a jumble of stray impulses and foolish desires

which come from outside stimuli or unchecked instinct. These take the place of deliberate decision governed by reason and go on to produce indecision, loss of will power (abulia), inconstancy and discouragement. Finally the higher level of consciousness loses control of the impulses which come from its lower subconscious levels. And the will loses control over the drives toward mere sense pleasure.

Too frequently life turns out to be agitated and restless, amusing, if you will, but sad and empty, tormented, anarchical. For some it is living without knowledge of how to rest peacefully or work efficiently. For others it is ignorance of how to have a real desire, or how to dominate feelings or the sexual instinct. For many it is a life empty of interior happiness and, at least for some, merely a heap of diversions and pastimes.

This book has been written in the hope of alleviating, in some part, such burdens and to give some guidance in the re-education of control. It is primarily the fruit of the author's own personal experience.

In the first place it is meant for those who are fatigued from excessive work, worries or sufferings. Possibly they may have lost control of their thoughts and so will not know how to rest or sleep peacefully; or they may be unable to control their fears or sadness. The first part of the book is intended especially for this group.

Secondly, we are writing for those who are healthy of mind but who wish greater efficiency in studies or business, greater energy and constancy in carrying out plans, greater control of feelings or instincts, more joy, satisfaction and interior happiness. These

will find useful and practical advice especially in
the second part of the book.

Further, we are also writing for educators and
directors of souls who meet up with problem cases
regarding study or virtue. These problems often
arise because of mental wandering, inefficiency, indecision or even laziness of will. Difficulties may also
come from uncontrolled passions, unreasonable fears,
or feelings of inferiority.

In the arrangement of the book our purpose is,
first of all, to be practical, to make it easier for you,
our readers, to get quick control of your nervous and
mental energies. The upshot of this will be greater
efficiency in work and greater mental health. We
want also to be accessible, even for non-specialists,
in order to lessen mental sufferings and help those
who need orientation or advice in their work or
studies. We want, too, to save time for you. Hence
we unify our teachings, condense explanations, make
résumés of them and include outline diagrams or
charts at the end of each chapter. We want, further,
to focus your attention especially on mental fatigue,
mental weakness, insufficient control and the internal difficulties which these cause. In practical applications we limit ourselves to the more immediate
results of acquired control. And, finally, we want to
interweave aphorisms or maxims which are educa-
tive and healthily optimistic. Once you engrave
these on your mind by repetition, they will help to
increase your health, efficiency and happiness.

July 31, 1963

Table of Contents

PART ONE

·

Happiness and Our Equipment for It

I

False and True Happiness

On the façade of the palace of pseudo-happiness we read invitations to pleasures, riches, fun; but happiness is not there. Echoes whisper to us from deep in its interior: "Vacuum, upset, disgust." Riches do not satisfy; they did not satisfy the eighty millionaires who committed suicide in the United States in one year. Nor should we confuse pleasure with happiness. By equivalating them, many have surrendered to vice, and found degradation, disgust, sickness, remorse, premature death and a likelihood of eternal damnation. Amusements and rounds of entertainment promise but do not bring us real fulfillment. There are so many young people who live without an ideal and feel deeply the vacuum of their lives. They would have done well to fill their lives with the satisfaction of duty done, or sacrifice for a noble cause. But they are satisfied to mask it with a series of amusements or drown it in coarse laughter or wild excitement. None of these roads lead to happiness.

True happiness is like a noble lady, calm and collected, who dwells in the interior of the soul's castle, knowing her real treasures and growing in appreciation of them. She is often seen externally through the window of the face when she clothes the human face with a smile. Her smile is the bright vesture of a rational being, something had neither by the animals nor the most beautiful flowers.

In this description we distinguish happiness (which is an intimately personal thing, tranquil, deep, and based on a certain nobility) from an alleged happiness which is really false, turbulent, and base. In it we list its three psychical elements: the factors of thought, will and feelings. And we mention its physiological counterpart, the human smile. Now to explain this briefly and summarize it in a schematic formula.

Happiness is *noble*. The true variety is not to be found in vice, anything degrading, or any illicit pleasures. Fast upon the sparkling sensation follows a lasting and bitter vacuum.

Happiness is *calm and collected*. There is no happiness in agitation and chaos. Happiness is found in the innermost part of a rational being. It is a deep satisfaction and unshakeable peace. It is not built upon riches, pleasures or power. Often there is more peace and joy among the comparatively poor than among the rich and the mighty. Many millionaires, crushed with worries, have grown old before their time.

Happiness is not caused by external events. For the same outcome may bring resignation, peace and joy to some, and sad despair to others.

The Lady of the castle knows and appreciates her real treasures and increases them. Here we have the three physical factors in true happiness. The first factor has to do with our *mind* or *thoughts*. By it we know or think about the great good had or soon to be had by us, and about the ways to increase it. The second factor is *volitional* or *executive*. By it we preserve and even increase that treasure. The third factor is connected with our feelings and emotions. By it we feel and appreciate our treasures. (Chapters III, IV, and V follow from this.)

The above we reduce to an outline-diagram as follows:

1. Happiness Formula

Prerequisite: a treasure in our secure possession.

Constituents: { thought about "the treasure";
will to hold and increase it;
feeling of satisfaction in it.

Fulfillment: the external expression of joy: a smile.

2. Happiness Formula

To live	:	Beauty, Truth, Goodness, Grace
In the present	:	not the past, nor the future
With unity	:	of thought and action
And fullness	:	of satisfaction, peace, and security

It is a matter of *living*, really living. The nobler and more active the life, the greater its happiness. It is not to be a kind of Buddhist Nirvana which offers edification, but mutilates the life of the spirit and annihilates all activity. Life in the present is a treasure possessed, and future life a treasure to be had, one we need to make us truly happy. For its sake we can take possession of the world of color, shape and sound, let it enter deep into our mind and impress itself on our affections and feelings. To this end we must receive sensations with full consciousness. (Cf. part B in Chapter III.)

And we must live *goodness*. This is an active

process—loving others and making them happy, loving God above all. There is also a passive aspect to it: feeling the love and goodness of others, and the love of God pouring itself out upon us.

Finally, for those of us who have faith, we must live the life of grace, activate it, increase it. The life of grace divinizes us and makes us able to do what is more than human, able to attain a happiness which is more than human.

We must live in the *present moment*. This is the only moment within our hands, the only one that can make us happy. The past exists no more; let us leave it to the divine mercy. And, though it does not yet exist, let us entrust the future to God's loving providence and live happily in the present. The "present" is a narrow track drawn between two chasms—the "past" and the "future." If a man falls by sadness or scrupulosity into the "past" or sinks by worry into the "future," he stops advancing toward his happiness. We must live the "present" in a *unity* of thought and action. Mental unity and concentration bring efficiency and joy (Chapter III). Whenever a man has many things to think about or do at the same time, he becomes nervous, upset, worried, but not happy.

Above all we must live in the present with a *fullness* of satisfaction, peace and joy. Full satisfaction depends upon our making real, at the present moment, what is most noble and most useful. For then we are getting the greatest possible return out of the present. This happens when we make acts of the virtues and perform our duty. In the concrete we thus carry out the will of God, the ideal of Infinite Wisdom. And if this satisfaction is founded on a pure and peaceful conscience and a sense of security in possessing such a great good, then we have happiness. It is a limited happiness, but a true one. It is as deep a one as can be had in this life. And it can be had even in the midst of sorrow or pain. This will become, in the next life, completely full and limitless, without any possibility then of suffering.

But these two happiness formulas are impossible for those who look for happiness in vice, vanity or disorder. These formulas are difficult for many victims of the lack of control in modern life.

II

Re-Education for Happiness

WHOEVER LOOKS FOR HAPPINESS where it is not to be found—in vice, vanity or disorder—will have to begin by adjusting his life to the ways of duty and virtue. Books about morality and the life of the spirit will teach him how to do this, especially if he also gets personal advice from some head wiser than his own. In this book we aim to help the many people of good will who actually are on the right track, but are not so happy as they should be. Either they do not understand or do not use correctly the mental (psychical) equipment which would give them unity and fulness of life at the present moment.

Some lack a clear precision in their use of the senses. They do not pay real attention to what they see or do. So they block off from entering within them the peace and joy of really conscious sensations or esthetic pleasure. Others subject themselves to excessive fatigue. Others let their mental life go wandering all over the place. So they find no rest or depth in their thoughts. And they do not experience the joy and efficiency that would come from orderly mental work. Still others are indecisive or fickle. They do not know how to use the immense force of their will. Finally, many others experience antipathies and repugnance, attractions and inclinations that obsess them and draw them still further away from duty. Or the breakdown of their emotional life is seen in excessive feelings of sadness, fear or disgust. The conclusion of all this is that we have to know how to use these four factors in the life of our spirit correctly. Control in the use of them will increase our happiness.

The following paragraphs on emotional machinery give more details about the symptoms, causes, and remedies for this lack of mental and emotional control which blocks happiness. In such a brief outline there is no attempt to include the whole sweep of the problem of psychical or psychosomatic troubles. Still less does it mark out the frontiers between the physical and spiritual; so often these overlap and intermix. What follows is a pedagogical outline of the sufferings which are a consequence of insufficient control. It is a bird's-eye view of the problem.

EMOTIONAL MACHINERY

The *occasion* of the emotion may be any happening reaching the cerebral cortex through our senses or memory. The *cause* is the interpretation we give to the event as related to our happiness. If we consider it as an obstacle, we tend to destroy it: anger. If it is a danger, we try to escape from it: fear. If it is a loss: sadness.

The thoughts which produce anger may be "I, He, It." "I, who am so good, I cannot tolerate such a treatment." "He is bad," or "They are bad." "It (the happening) is intolerable." Fear is caused by: "A

great danger is imminent and unavoidable." Sadness
is caused by "My loss is total, irreparable."

These thoughts, as an alarm call, reach the hypothalamus which is the engine room of emotions. The
hypothalamus, through the autonomous nervous
system, sets the organism in a fighting attitude
(muscular tension). Such tension, when intense or
repeated, may affect some weak part of the organism
and will cause pallor, headache, lump in the throat,
pain the back of the neck, hyperventilation, dizziness, heart or stomach trouble, ulcer-like or gall-
bladder-like pain, fibrositis, neurodermatitis, and
many other functional diseases.

More intense or conscious emotion.—Being aware
of the commotion, if our reason judges it as unnecessary and the stimulus as unimportant, peace will
return. But if we let loose our imagination, this will
command full attention to its fears, hatred or sadness with a possibility of fixations, obsessions, exaggerations and transfers, and still stronger feelings
and impulses. Such a repeated and stronger stimulation of the hypothalamus, or the first stimulus itself,
when considered as important, introduces new forces
into the battle for happiness, namely the glands with
their powerful hormones.

The pituitary gland in depressive emotions releases
an excess of the somatotrophic hormone (S.T.H.)
which may produce high blood pressure, arthritis,
asthma, fatigue, etc. In aggressive emotions there is
an excess of ACTH, the adreno-cortico-trophic hormone, which activates the cortex of the adrenal
glands.

Thence 26 hormones, which influence the mineral

and glucose metabolism, will flow from the cortex of the glands; and from their medulla, which has a nervous connection with the hypothalamus, adrenalin will come out immediately. Their excess may end in ulcer, diabetes, malnutrition, infection, hypertension, insomnia, etc.

To avoid so many diseases and *to control* our emotions, we may:

1) Change the external expression of the eyes, voice, respiration, and muscles.

2) Avoid the thought which produces the emotion, either avoiding the occasion, or thinking about something interesting, or having conscious sensations or a pleasant occupation.

3) Bring in the opposite thought, discovering the good side of persons, happenings and sorrows.

4) Bring in the opposite feeling and tendency in order to counteract the negative inclinations to insecurity, aversion or sadness. Do that through acts, thoughts and attitudes of courage, heroism, sympathy, love, optimism, joy, etc.

In a nutshell: Be happy and healthy by positive, pleasant thoughts even in adversity. These will cause positive emotions, and such emotions and your smiling eyes will help keep or restore your health and spray rays of happiness around you.

To comprehend the foregoing better, a good procedure will be to enter into the psychology of victims of the illness by listening to their own description of it. (Three case histories will shortly follow and more of them will be found throughout the book.) Unfortunately in the accelerated life of our age these victims are legion. They are recruited daily and not very often found among intellectual or affective nonentities. For these latter do not usually have the exuberance of mental life that is a prerequisite of swinging to an extreme and losing control. More often we see them among thinkers, writers and men of parts, among persons of exquisite sensibilities, among ambitious and talented students. How many lecturers, writers and professors of international fame have in our day been struck down by "overwork." Newton, for example, admitted that he could not work more than two hours a day. Even Dr. Vittoz, the psychotherapist, began by curing himself. And so it should not be a shameful or depressing thing to declare oneself mentally fatigued.

"At the age of twenty," a student describes himself, "despite an insatiable love of books, I suddenly found it impossible for me to study. Ten minutes of reading or writing brought on the most distressing feeling of fatigue. There was pain and, more frequently, a feeling of heat around the head and eyes. I simply could not drive off this sensation and concentrate on other ideas. A confusing succession of thoughts so oppressed me that I did not know how to control them. They were usually sad memories of the past, or painful anticipations of future misfortunes. They were sometimes so burdensome that I could not wholly drive them away by seeking refuge in conversation, walking or even manual labor. The most intimate part of my soul seemed split in two. I felt as if another part of me were overcoming the conscious part of me. Gradually I sank into discouragement, worry, feelings of inferiority and indecision. At times there was a swift transition from optimism to pessimism, from joy to sadness, without any objective cause. I 'was on an open road to all sorts of phobias, fear of appearing in public, incipient dizzy spells and scruples of conscience.

"A little later I fell prey to insomnia. My time of rest brought me no true repose. My sleep was interrupted by dreams and nightmares. When I got up I would find that I was more tired than when I went to bed. The illness and my sadness increased, yet those closest to me misunderstood it. When they saw me apparently strong and physically robust, some diagnosed that the illness came from my imagination. Others more charitably, but not more scientifically, tried to persuade me to do what I so anxiously wished to do, that is, not to be worried, not to be absent-minded, not to fear, to control myself. But they did not show me *how* to do it. It was as if you were to advise a person suffering from a fit of coughing or vomiting simply not to cough, not to vomit, without telling him the means to employ.

"I went through ten years of this. But after six months of exercises for mental re-education I triumphed over all those difficulties. Now I have almost forgotten that I had been ill. Although I have not yet recovered the same full capacity for work as heretofore, I do find that I am cured and satisfied."

I, too, the author, had to pass through that sorry state of distressing introspection. Yet it was useful. For my own pattern of mental activity was developed and illuminated first by the knowledge and advice of the famous Jesuit psychologist, Fr. Laburu.[1] It was afterwards completed and systematized in

---

[1] Professor of Scientific Questions at the Gregorian University (Rome).

Lausanne by Dr. Arthus, according to the precepts of Dr. Vittoz.

They gave me the key to my cure in the re-education of control. This method I have confirmed by study and wide experience with the sick. It has taught me how to direct and console those who are suffering from illnesses similar to mine. I say "to direct and console," for we should not prescind from medical aid. Even if symptoms seem to be alike, they sometimes have far deeper roots. In such cases only consultation with a spiritual psychiatrist could promise security and improvement.

"I am eighteen years old," a student once wrote to me, "and formerly I was as strong as an oak. I could read for hours and hours without fatigue. I was very optimistic and felt capable of any undertaking. But last term I studied very little and had a lot of fun with various companions. As examination time drew near we spent several nights studying until three o'clock in the morning. We drove off sleepiness by means of coffee. But now that the examinations are over, I hardly know what has happened to me. Sleep is a torment. It is either a network of images or else a single image which continually repeats itself. Even during the day my head boils. I cannot pay attention to conversation. Reading tires me. I cannot distract myself. Life terrifies me; I am afraid of everything, even of myself."

This young man lost control because of excess and disorder in his mental work. Let such a one take heart, begin to strengthen his overexcited nervous system, perhaps travel a bit and rest. Then let him begin the work of mental re-education. Let us form ourselves without waiting for somebody else to form and model us. See, for example, how children amuse themselves when they are alone. They build structures of clay or sand which they then enjoy leveling to the ground; so should we in solitude mold our characters and virtues, and destroy our defects.

Four everyday duties will help me to achieve a healthier mental life. I must resolve, first, to strengthen and govern my body (nourishment, exercise and discipline); secondly, to feed and enlighten my intellect (serious, concentrated work); thirdly, to elevate and control my heart (love of God and neighbor); and finally, to strengthen and exercise my will (decision and constancy).

III

Receptive and Productive
Mental Activity

IN ORDER TO ATTAIN MENTAL mastery man should be capable of governing the kingdom of his mind, of opening or shutting its gates by receiving or rejecting thoughts at will. This mental activity is twofold: the mind receives sensations like a photographic camera or radio receiver, in which case the attention is gentle and almost passive; but it also produces images, ideas and reasoning processes like a movie projector or radio transmitter. Whether these are consciously or unconsciously elaborated, this is active or creative attention.

We base re-education upon the distinction between the receiving and producing powers of our mental world. Our axiom is that we cannot be fully both receiving and producing at the same time.

RECEPTIVE POWER

Receptive power is exercised when we receive conscious sensations. This means not only to stimulate our senses through noise, smells, hardness, and so forth, and to send nervous currents to our brain centers, but also to put more life into our sensations, receiving them consciously and filing them away in memory.

When distractions do not frustrate them from without and our secret thoughts do not tamper with them from within, conscious sensations are a tonic for the brain and the nervous system. They bring peace, joy, tranquillity and repose. They allow nature to work. Through them the objective world created by God enters within us with all its beauty. For if you know how to receive it within yourself, you will obtain joy from the blue of the sky, peace of a starry night, beauty and variety of flowers, freshness of morning air, whisper of a fountain, whistling of wind, greenness of fields, trilling of birds, songs of innocent children.

Re-Education of Receptive Power

Many persons rarely have clear sensations. This is especially true of the emotionally disturbed. They live in their own subjective world which is sad and unreal. Only rarely do they come out into the exterior world, beautiful and joyful as it was created by God. And even when they do, their sensations are modified by extraneous or subjective thoughts. To these people we offer the following advice.

For your re-education you should apply your sense of sight for about ten or twenty seconds to a landscape, an object, a detail. Keep a tranquil or almost passive attention. Take your time. Consider the object before you and no other. Pay no attention to any other idea. Let the object enter within you as it is in itself, without any special effort. Look at it the way a young child does. Take care that the muscles of forehead and eyes are loose and relaxed. When your nerves and muscles are tense, it is easy to have mental tension also. This results in lack of peace in the act of vision. But if your muscles relax, your mind also tends to rest.

Apply your hearing to a near or distant noise. Let yourself be penetrated by the sounds as above, naturally, without mental discussion of the fact or its cause. Be a mere receiver of sound and perceive it with pleasure and relaxation.

Apply touch by feeling objects, their coldness, heat, hardness and so on. Feel your own footsteps, the chair on which you are resting, the door opening. Feel your own breathing, the air entering your chest and filling it. The first sensation perceived will be the most conscious.

Walking Consciously.—This exercise is very useful for resting as well as for overcoming agoraphobia (that is, a morbid fear of crossing an open space or being out in the open). It also counteracts attacks of incipient dizziness. Hence we shall describe it in greater detail.

First get a separate sensation or clear consciousness of your foot being put down, your leg moving and your whole body sliding forward. Then coordinate these sensations and unite them to the rhythm of your breathing and to visual and auditory perception. You will then have a feeling of freedom and security.

Practicing Conscious Sensations.—If you are haunted by these troubles or by dizziness, exercise yourself in these sensations several times morning

and afternoon. Do them, for example, on five different occasions. Each time spend about five minutes
on them and receive five or more sensations through
each sense.[1]

Try to experience, as far as possible, the truth in
the old maxim, "*Age quod agis*"; that is, "Attend to
what you are doing," or "Do what you're doing." But
you must do all this as if in sport, with no anxiety,
fear or worry.

In a few days you will notice a greater peace and
joy. The world will appear more beautiful. It will,
as a matter of fact, impress you as it really is in
itself. It will not be colored by your uncontrolled
unconsciousness.

A very depressed person once made this state-
ment to me: "After ten days of conscious sensations I feel myself another man. The world seems
joyful and beautiful to me." Previously he had been
looking at it through the prism of his sad thoughts.
Or rather, he had been looking at it, but had not
seen it. Many people have been cured by this
exercise alone.

Chinese painters, we are told, retire to a mountain
before actually painting in order to contemplate and
feel nature. They let it enter into themselves in all
its beauty. Afterwards they transfer it to their can-
vas just as they sensed it. That is why their pictures
have so much life and feeling. To allow exterior
beauty to enter into oneself is characteristic of
painters and poets.

---

[1] Follow the same norm in the concentration and will exercises.
Do them the same number of times morning and afternoon. Each
time do each exercise about five times in order to form a healthy
habit.

PRODUCTIVE POWER

Under this heading we include ideas, images, associations of ideas and reasoning processes. These may be produced voluntarily or spontaneously by the unconscious. This "production" is active attention, work. This is the normal cause of fatigue which varies according to the kind of concentration.

Concentration

When we follow the course of one idea to the exclusion of every other, when we are attentive only to what we are studying or hearing and forget everything else, even ourselves, then the intellectual return is at its maximum. Then natural pleasure is great, and there is only that minimal fatigue which we call physical. Two hours of this perfect attention are equalized by five minutes of rest through conscious sensations ("receiving"). A day's work is balanced by a night's sleep. Thus we can work intensely at a single idea for many years, and intense and orderly study, far from weakening the brain, is a gymnastic which strengthens it.

Imperfect Attention.—Our attention is poor when we follow out one idea with another idea or image constantly interrupting it. This we call a distraction. Then the return and satisfaction are less and fatigue greater.

Our attention is harmful to us when we follow out several ideas simultaneously. This happens, for example, when we are reading or listening to an explanation or discourse and at the same time we attend to another parasite idea (worry, fear, sensa-

tion of fatigue, scruples). The fatigue is then dis-
proportionate, abnormal. We call this mental fatigue.
Then we grasp ideas less deeply and forget them
sooner. The distraction, or parasite idea, has an
effect like that when two typewriter keys are both
touched at the same time. The machine resists and
the writing is confused. So our brain becomes
fatigued and we understand ideas but poorly, and
we can have no experience of satisfaction or joy. A
quarter of an hour's work is not equalized by another
quarter hour's rest. A whole night is not enough to
make up for the day's expenditure of energy. This
is why we are exhausted from a hurried visit to a
museum or after nervously rushing through the news-
paper. If this type of labor is continued it leads at
last to "overwork" (fatigue of the brain) and
"breakdowns."

Geniuses of one sort or another—artists, inventors,
heroes, saints—are usually silent, concentrated. Dissi-
pation weakens by dispersing energies; concentration
gathers them together, as it were, in a close bundle.

According to a new theory, imperfect concentration is often responsible for some visual defects or
indistinct vision due to bad focusing. When the
accommodation nerves of the eyeball are taxed by
divided or imperfect attention, they put into a state
of excessive tension the muscles which lengthen or
shorten for the purpose of focusing upon the object.
With time these muscles lose the elasticity which is
necessary for accommodating the eye to vision.

That is the reason why many nervous people, by
practicing the *Age quod agis* ("Do what you're
doing"), improve their concentration and often find
that their vision also is bettered.

Causes of Defective Concentration—
1. Bodily weakness. 2. Nervous and muscular tension. 3. Lack of training or bad training of the attention. 4. Some emotional disturbance, a fear or desire which pulls all thought into its wake. This is the most frequent cause.

Re-Education of Productive Power

In addition to strengthening of the body to counteract weakness, and relaxation exercises to counteract tension, re-education will be twofold. One phase will be more mechanical and technical, the other more mental. Let us take up the former first.

Everyone, even the mentally ill, can concentrate his attention for a moment of time. Beginning with this possibility and graduating the exercises, he can arrive at normal concentration.

The exercises here proposed are not the only ones nor are these particular exercises absolutely necessary. But they have as guarantee the experience of the old school of psychotherapy at Lausanne. They may be omitted by persons whose problem is not one of increasing the productive power of concentration or by those for whom the exercises of conscious sensations, as outlined previously, suffice. Whatever other method may help the victim to get out of himself and fix his attention on other ideas will be advantageous. This will be especially true if he finds it useful and pleasant.

*External Visual Concentration.—*If you make a dot and think of nothing else, you will have an instant's concentration. If you prolong it in a straight line without thinking of anything else, you will attain a concentration of some seconds. With your finger, then, trace in the air several large figures without interrupting their continuity. Follow them attentively. Make, for example, each of the figures below five times each.

A student came to me one day with the complaint of great mental wandering in his study. There was

Figure 1

no particular focus-point around which his distractions would come and go. He began to do these exercises for about five minutes in the morning, again at noon, in the afternoon and at night. In four days he could do them naturally and without distractions. He then went on to do the ones illustrated below. They are a bit more difficult and demand a more prolonged attention.

Figure 2

I also taught him to trace in the air giant capital letters and whole words in which there was no break in the continuity, always watching his finger with tranquil attention. After ten days of this somewhat artificial education he was able to leave these crutches behind and apply his attention to the book he was studying. He easily succeeded in making résumés of short paragraphs, then longer passages and even a half-page at a single reading.

A businessman was on the verge of a collapse because of excessive work and the nervous tension under which he was living. He went to Dr. George W. Hall, an eminent neurologist. After the diagnosis was made that there was no acute organic lesion of any kind, he asked for a treatment which would permit him to reknit as soon as possible the rhythms of his accelerated life. Dr. Hall suggested that he have an aquarium of tropical fish built in his private office and that he spend an hour every day peacefully watching the graceful convolutions of those little creatures. The patient was a bit nonplussed, but followed the prescription faithfully. Before the year was out he sent a donation to Dr. Hall's hospital as a token of gratitude for his cure. The fish were tracing out the types of maneuvres which we here recommend.

Internal Visual Concentration.—It will sometimes be helpful to do the same maneuvres mentally, without the aid of your hand, as if upon a blackboard. Practice this, too, for several days.

Auditory Concentration.—We shall explain auditory concentration in the form of an actual case. One woman found it hard to follow spoken addresses or lectures. The effort to concentrate brought on such a nervous strain that several times she had to leave the hall. And a slight noise would awaken her at night. Whether at home or in the office she could not read or write if anyone were, for instance, to move about or play a piano in her vicinity.

For several days she exercised herself in voluntarily encouraging different kinds of noises. Then she would follow the sound of a clock, saying and hearing mentally, "Tick-tock, tick-tock," for about ten times with perfect concentration. On the second day she reached fifteen and on the fourth more than twenty without a thought of anything else. To this exercise she gave at the most only five minutes each time. But she did it about eight times a day. Once she had satisfactorily obtained this auditory concentration, she went on to listen voluntarily to an address or lecture. At first she listened for ten, then fifteen minutes or more without fear or distractions. When these did come, her only care was to fix her attention anew on what was being said. In a month she was cured.

She also undertook to do these exercises in the midst of noise and other people's conversations. When she had no more fear of these difficulties and was no longer annoyed by the conversation of others, she could at last work peacefully and tranquilly.

Concentration in the Midst of Noise.—We recommend this same procedure to people who have to work amidst the racket of an office, or conversations or music, where the distractions are many and fatigue is so easily induced. They should practice for only a few minutes at first. Then they should do it for a longer time till they learn to be completely independent of what is going on around them. They should imitate children who can attend to their book or lesson without bothering about the shouts of their companions. It never occurs to children to make a protest against noise. In the sincere acceptance of noise is the main part of the remedy. This is also a good way to get to sleep.

Touch Concentration.—Preserve for a few seconds the sensation of hardness, cold, heat, and the like when you touch an object.

Concentration on Movement.—When walking, for example, realize now that the right foot is moving, now the left, then the whole body. For this exercise you will of course have to move slowly or you will be unable to feel those sensations.

Concentration on One Part of the Body.—Take your hand, for instance. Feel it as your own, as alive, while you hold it out before you. With a few days of practice you will after a few moments of concentration feel a slight prickling sensation in the part on which you are concentrating.

By this exercise Dr. Vittoz cured even some cases of paralysis which were of mental origin. For example, to move a paralyzed arm the patient first had to concentrate on one part of it. Then he changed the concentration from above to below, and vice versa. Finally the will could command movement again.

Concentration against Pain.—By the same method we can stop or lessen the feeling of pain from, say, an injury. By concentrating attention on the part affected by pain, *not on the pain itself or its causes*, a voluntary wave from within will neutralize the wave of pain from the injury outside. It will keep the pain, or most of it, from coming to the nerve centers and being felt.

A More Mental Form of Re-Education

Lack of interest in what we read, hear or do, or the greater repulsion, attraction or importance we give to what we desire or fear are the greatest enemies of concentration. Unreasonable fears or parasite ideas, worries or uncontrolled passions cause the most distractions. The remedy lies, as indicated above, in discovering their disturbing focus-point and then weakening and even destroying it. We shall explain this more at length in chapters V and X.

We must arouse interest and pleasure in what we are studying or doing by considering its utility, convenience and ease of performance. In a word, we should see it in the light and warmth of an ideal (see Chapter XV).

Concentration in Reading.—Fix your attention on what you are reading until you come to the first period. Rest there a few moments with conscious sensations. Read again as far as the second period and rest again, and so on until a page is completed. Repeat this exercise three times a day. This is an excellent method for re-education and is the best way to control excessive haste and anxiety to finish the reading. This haste and anxiety cause much fatigue. More concrete means for concentrating in study, in the case of healthy people as well as sick, will be found in my new work, *Mental Efficiency without Fatigue* (Joseph F. Wagner, Inc., New York).

Neuromuscular Relaxation.—We said before that neuromuscular tension is usually one of the causes of bad concentration, or may be produced by it. As a matter of fact, with all mental activity there is a corresponding bodily activity in nerves and muscles. Every excess or disorder in the first is accompanied by tension or fatigue in the second.

We have all observed muscular activity in external attitudes of attention. Some of these are eager movements, shortened breath, a slight bending forward of the head, stiffening of the shoulder muscles.

There are many nervous or tense people who easily tire themselves out if they read or study while seated. If, instead, they read or study while walking in a garden, they can keep at it much longer. This is true because there is muscular tension while they are seated. While walking, however, they can better relax their muscles, especially those used in breathing. There are also more frequent moments of receptivity or rest.

Another effect of excessive tension is a certain tendency to overactivity when we try to surpass ourselves in vivacity and effort. We then underestimate fatigue until prostration comes.

Practice.—If you notice this tension in yourself, use the following relaxing technique. Loosen well the muscles of your forehead (without wrinkling or knitting it). Then relax the muscles around your eyes (keep a tranquil gaze like that of a contemplative). Relax and loosen your mouth (tongue, jaws and lips). Then relax the muscles of hands and feet (let them be quiet and limp and, as it were, feel the weight of gravity). Relax especially the muscles of waist and diaphragm (let your breathing be natural, deep and rhythmical).

There is a residual tension which ordinarily remains in hypertense muscles even after the rest and relaxation of sleep. The best way to eliminate this is by rhythmic exercises of the arms and legs, bending and revolving the trunk, and exercises which make the joints more flexible.

You must, however, keep in mind that this technique will have less effect if the mental causes of tension remain within us. The mental cause is either insecurity with resulting fears or worries, or an excessive spirit of competition. These cause exaggerated effort and haste and are rooted in an overestimation of oneself. As a counterbalance to such tendencies, in addition to what we shall say in the chapters on feelings (Chapters V and X), we here point out the tonic and calming effects of friendship or love, a reasonable ideal and a firm religious faith together with a pure conscience.

If you have nothing to lean upon before facing the problems which each day brings, if you cannot find within yourself the equivalent of this support, you will be disturbed and tense. For the child an external support will be his mother's love. For a wife it will be her husband. For a youth it may be a faithful friend, a self-sacrificing teacher, or his spiritual director. And for the fervent believer it will be the help of God. One's own interior support or personal security will be strengthened by lending security or support to other people. Oftentimes widows triumph in life and spread security and joy as long as their children are small, yet feel sad, insecure and troubled when these children grow up. Give to others love, help and protection and you will increase your own security, joy and peace.

Excessive effort and haste disappear when we purge our ideal of strange rivalries or stratagems and accommodate it to our strength and possibilities (see Chapter XV). But even when you succeed in life and see your human ideal attained, there will still remain in the depths of your being a fountain of restlessness and tension. You can only remove this if, when you think about the future, you find in firm, religious faith and a pure conscience an answer which will give you peace.

A Fundamental Axiom

We said at the beginning that we cannot at the same time be both fully receptive and productive. We cannot have a clear consciousness of a sensation and at the same instant be thinking of something else. By our very thinking of this other thing we cease to have that clear consciousness. And, vice versa, in following out an idea and concentrating our attention on it, we cease to give clear attention to our sensations. In short, when the field of consciousness is wholly occupied by sensation, there is no room for other concentration, and vice versa.

One consoling conclusion is the possibility of resting and temporarily overcoming worries, sadness, phobias and passions. On the one hand only productive power can cause fatigue. On the other hand our receptive power can bring peace and rest. We cannot at the same time be wholly receptive and productive. But with a little training we can make ourselves merely receptive even under the influence of worries and phobias. So there follows the clear possibility of acquiring this repose and mental control by means of receptivity.

A priest once confided to me that with this means alone he succeeded in dominating an instinctive fear which he had had since childhood. "I was afraid," he told me, "of cemeteries at night. So I went to one after dark. I kept my attention continually on pious thoughts or conscious sensations. Thus I succeeded in not having the feeling of fear master me even for a minute, although several times it fought hard for entrance.

"In the same way I conquered impatience in treating with a very disagreeable person. Each time his irritating words and actions provoked me to anger, I turned my attention away from them. I concentrated on observing his mental patterns, his gestures, tone of voice, or the colors of things around us. It was a kind of mental armor which kept the explosive out."

By the same simple method of having conscious sensations when an evil impulse came, a complete cure was wrought for a man tempted impulsively to wrath and suicide. A notable improvement was brought in the same way to a young man with almost unrestrainable sexual obsessions or impulses.

FROM IMPERFECT MASTERY TO CONTROL

The mentally weak or sick have no true concentration when they work or study. And during the times when they should be resting, they go on thinking of their studies or business. Or they walk wrapped in worry, doubts or sadness. Even in sleep they attain no true repose. Instead they frequently pass the time in dreams. They produce much more than they receive. This may be graphically represented as in the following figure.

25% receptivity, rest

75% productivity, work, expenditure

Figure 3

By concentrated work at its proper time and sensations or conscious life at other times they can avoid disorder and attain the equilibrium of persons who are mentally normal. These latter, in moments of concentration or study, think only of what they are doing. They forget everything else. At other times they either have conscious sensations or think of nothing at all. In this way the time of rest or sensation is proportioned to the time of work or concentration. Their balance of activity is pictured in the following graph.

50%—12 hrs. for sleep, recreation, rest, etc.

50%—12 hrs. of study, work, productivity, etc.

Figure 4

Mental Control

We should attain such dominion over our faculties that we can pass swiftly from work to rest, from our interior world to the exterior, from concentration to sensation and vice versa, changing from graph A to B (following).

In A the shift from work to rest comes with a

period of intermediate agitation, with fluctuations of work.

In *B* the transition from concentration to sensation is fast and immediate, without fluctuations or intermediate states.

To attain this control it will help to pass the hand of a clock mentally from one hour to another. Inter-

Figure 5

pose conscious sensations after concentrating on each hour for a few seconds.

Figure 6

Do the exercise this way. Say "Twelve o'clock" and imagine the hand on twelve. Concentrate your attention there. Then rest with a few sensations. Then say "One o'clock" and mentally shift the hand from XII to I. Concentrate and rest as before. Thus cover this half of the clock in one or two minutes of intermittent concentration. Do this exercise, also, three times a day.

Use these exercises to produce a healthful habit of rest, conscious life and concentration. They directly attack mental vagueness, excess and disorder. They must be done methodically and constantly by dedicating to them several times a day a few minutes which are free from every other occupation. *Without having put them into practice you will find it hard to understand the utility of this part of the book.* Be careful in these exercises to avoid anything which is negative or depressing. Instead of reminding us of our illness or deficiency, they should help us to forget it. They should convince us that we are controlling our illness by making us take more joy in the present and in the real world. They shall make us feel that we have more freedom and have greater mastery of ourselves. Perform them, then, with zest, as a sort of mental sport, without worry or anxiety, without attributing to them a greater efficacy than they have.

Maximum Normal Concentration Period

Fixed and clear concentration on a single sensation or idea, without repeating the impulse to pay attention to it, will only last a few seconds, scarcely half a minute. Yet you can pay attention to successive sensations or reasoning processes for a longer time. All in all, our maximum effort at concentration will normally last about twenty minutes. We do not exceed this without placing an unnecessary strain on ourselves. We must then rest for an instant and relax our attention. This is what we do instinctively when turning the page of a book or changing our position.

This is why we should interrupt our reading after fifteen or twenty minutes and take a few moments of rest by conscious sensations. Hence, also, the pedagogical necessity in lectures or sermons, especially if we are talking to children, of relaxing the audience's attention with a digression, story or joke. If we do not grant the audience this rest they will take it for themselves and thus lose the thread of our discourse. In this as in most matters difficulties should be reasons for greater courage and energy, not excuses for sloth or cowardice. Just as a tree grows more luxuriantly beneath the pruning knife, so our spirit becomes stronger and more agile with the struggle.

OUTLINE DIAGRAM

✦➤◦⟨✦

Mental Activity and Re-Education

MENTAL ACTIVITY

- **RECEPTIVE**
  - **What it is**
    - receiving successive sensations into consciousness
    - a kind of passive attention
  - **Effects**
    - peace, rest, tonic, joy
  - **Re-education**
    - conscious sensations
    - conscious acts
- **PRODUCTIVE**
  - **What it is**
    - producing images, reasoning processes
    - active attention
  - **Efficient**
    - concentration on one idea only
    - minimal "physical" fatigue
    - maximum return
  - **Defective**
    - attention with distractions
    - greater fatigue
    - less return
  - **Harmful**
    - following several ideas at once
    - harmful effects on vision
    - causes
      - maximum fatigue
      - minimum return
  - **Re-education**
    - sensual
      - visual concentration
      - concentration on sound and touch
      - concentration on one part of the body
    - mental
      - concentration in reading
      - removing worries
      - arousing interest
    - neuromuscular relaxation
- **Fundamental axiom**
  - you do not produce and receive simultaneously
  - so learn to rest and control yourself
- **From imperfect mastery to control**
  - equilibrium through
  - rapid transition
  - from concentration to sensation
- **Maximum concentration period**

IV

Acts of the Will

" 'I will' is a phrase rarely meant though much in use. A man who comes to realize the secret of really using his will, though today he be poor and lonely, will soon surpass all others."—Lacordaire

DEFINITION

THE WILL is a rational appetite which tends toward the good, once the good is apprehended by our intellect. It is also the executive power of our personality by which we choose and pursue definite goals and the means to those goals. Accommodated to mental treatment, the will may be described as an individual energy by which we are able freely to organize the representation of an act and freely to determine its execution. The greatest of our mental energies, it will, if well channeled, most quickly cure us. This energy is accumulated in deliberation and discharged in decision. It is distinct from our acts. It is free, active and guided by intelligence.

Even in the case of people with nervous and emotional disturbances and conflicts, even in cases of apparent loss of will power, this energy still exists though latent and unused.

False or Ineffective Acts of the Will

Ineffectual desire: passive, necessary; the presentation of a good object suffices for our will to desire it.

Vague intention, or "having a mind to do something": this is a kind of tendency to do something; it is not even wanting it, but a vague plan or attempt to want it.

Impulse: this is being determined by external circumstances or forces; it is indeliberate, instinctive, a great force but a chaotic one.

Velleity: this is an absence of the feeling of personality; "I would like to," but not "I will."

Effective Acts of the Will

Those acts truly and fully come from our will which leave us with the persuasion and intimate conviction that they are free.

This kind of act truly educates the will. It leads most quickly to a cure. Its source is will power. This is the "deliberate determination" of which St. Ignatius Loyola, founder of the Society of Jesus, speaks in his book, *The Spiritual Exercises.*

Theory of Dr. Vittoz

This theory, not yet substantiated, bases its description of this act of will upon what he claimed he was able to feel when placing his hand lightly on a patient's forehead.

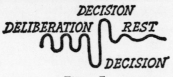

Figure 7

First he felt the pulsations, as he says, which reflect deliberation. They are similar to those of perfect concentration. Then there are one or several stronger waves which correspond to decision or discharge of the will. Finally there is the smooth rhythm of repose.

Dr. Vittoz and his students, by their refined sense of touch, perceived "brain pulsations" which they distinguished from the ordinary pulse. These they found useful for the external observation and control of a patient's mental acts.

Their distinction and classification, done "grosso modo" by the Lausanne school, confirms and synthesizes what has been explained above.

Figure 8

Note that these graphic representations of the waves give us, in their general pattern, the immediate impression that conscious sensations are a tonic activity of our mental system and produce rest.

Secondly, note that defective "production," or simultaneous work at several ideas, disturbs, fatigues and weakens us.

Finally, as pictured in the will curve, decision produces peace and rest. Indecision, on the contrary, is a source of fatigue. For the brain then overloads itself with energies which find no outlet.

Requisites for True Acts of the Will

1. Make the act concrete.—Picture clearly to yourself what you are going to do. Concentrate your attention on this image. The more detailed and vivid an image you form, the more force it will have. Lack of this requisite is a prime source of lack of will power in people with emotional or nervous disturbances. It is hard for them to halt the flow of their ideas. Their productive power does not obey them thoroughly. They find it hard to concentrate on what they are going to do.

To concentrate well on what you plan to do, answer the following questions: "What am I going to do? When must it be done? How?" Consider also the other conditions necessary for execution. Our most noble faculty is not put in motion when it does not know where it is going. Because of this lack of precision many pretended plans do not pass from the stage of desire, or velleity or incipient intention. There is no mental discharge in them. Here we have the main cause of inefficiency in what we thought were decisions. They were too vague, not concrete.

2. Feel the possibility of execution.—The queen of our faculties is too conscious of its dignity to throw itself consciously into a frustration. It will not exert a force which it knows must be sterile. Once the act is made concrete, examine yourself to see whether the energy you possess is equal to the energy necessary for the act. You should feel this possibility somewhat as an athlete feels whether he has the needed muscular strength to perform some feat.

3. *Have a motive.*—Our will is an energy ruled by intelligence and naturally inclined toward the good. You should perceive values, goods, motives for an act. To obtain strength of will these motives should be:

> *Objective:* good in themselves, not merely because of other considerations.
>
> *Subjective:* perceived as good for you.
>
> *Accommodated* to your individual capacity. This will be more the motive of sensible pleasure for the young, more the motive of abstract goodness for adults.
>
> *Actuated* or *recorded:* either put into action at the very moment of decision, or stored up for the moment decided upon for execution.

4. *Make a sincere will act or decision.*—This is the condition most frequently absent and causing most failures of will. It consists in really determining yourself. Decision converts a plan to present or future reality. Decision makes a real actuality of what is merely possible. By decision you give the victory to a practical idea by excluding the opposite or alternatives as if impossible for you. By this sincerity you *feel* that the "Yes" or "No" is true, effective, certain. You are left with the conviction that the object of your act of will must be realized

and that its existence is already assured. The deep rooted cause of our weakness and impotency is in the slackness of our willing. When something is really willed, then hitherto unsuspected energies are released even by weak organisms.

RE-EDUCATION OF THE WILL

Those who are abulic (that is, those who suffer loss of will power) because of not making true acts of the will lose the internal consciousness or feeling for them. *They should above all practice simple acts which are thoroughly willed* (for example, walking, lifting their arm, touching some object) until they recapture the internal feeling of a will act. They should then go on graduating these acts from what is easier to the more difficult.

One young man, though educated in Catholic schools, threw over every moral restraint when he went on to the university. By habitually surrendering to impure vice he ended up in such a state of abulia and indecision that to him it seemed impossible to practice continence. He felt depressed, enslaved and annihilated in his personality. The vicious obsession was moreover obstructing his concentration in study.

It was not too hard to convince him that by reeducating his will he could remake his personality and recover his onetime vigor. In the first week of treatment he made external acts of the will eight or ten times each day by answering the following questions:

(1) *"What's up? When and how is it to be done?"*
    And he would make a concrete answer: The

question is whether or not "to get up out of bed, walk to the right or left," and so forth.

(2) *"Is this possible for me?* If I order my feet to take me to such and such a position, will they obey me?" And he got himself to feel the feasibility of this by making affirmative replies. When a somewhat more difficult matter would come up, he would say in a tone of absolute certainty: "Yes, I am sure I can do it!"

(3) *"Are there motives for willing this?* Yes, even if it be no more than to exercise my personality and educate myself."

(4) *"In that case shall I will it or not? Yes or No?"* And he would make the decision internally, setting aside the contrary possibility.

He experienced so much pleasure at feeling the strength of his will that on the third day he came to tell me all about it. Then he exercised himself in acts that were more difficult and required a greater conquest. Afterwards he practiced acts in which his passion was involved; for example, instead of going into such and such a dangerous place, he would go into another. Or he would order his eyes to fix themselves on some inoffensive object instead of an exciting one. And so on.

After sixteen days he was transformed. He had won the fight. He felt himself strong, joyful and happy. He left all his bad companions. The ideal of scholarship shone anew for him. He recovered ease of concentration. And I should add that to these mental means he added the supernatural one. He also reconciled himself with God in the Sacrament of Penance.

Anyone can use this system to increase his efficiency. All he need do is exercise himself in easy external will acts. Later he should go on to more difficult acts and then to internal acts. For example, you will to think about this thing or that. When such and such an idea or fear comes to you, decide now to think of or do such and such a certain, definite thing.

The greatest enemy to will power is the *indecision* common to all such victims. There is a struggle between practical ideas. Shall they act or not? Shall they do this or that? They do not know how to grant victory to one contesting choice and put an end to all discussion by excluding other possibilities. They should be able to correct this quickly.

EXECUTION

Decision introduces a great force into consciousness which carries it naturally onward toward act. If you can perform the act immediately, then this force is discharged without a new intervention of consciousness. If the execution is for some future time, the order will be transmitted and reserves of energy will remain on the subconscious level. They will be ready to work automatically at the proper time unless you intervene with a counter-order or some unforeseen obstacle occurs.

For example, I decide to go visit a friend after dinner. As a matter of fact I take my hat, board the streetcar and ride until I arrive at his house without making a new conscious act.

There are people who decide to rise at a determined time, and then the subconscious which never sleeps arouses them at the exact hour. It will even do this before the hour if they are worried about it.

Once you have decided that you must accept a certain practical idea, and have excluded the opposite as impossible, never discuss it at the time of execution. This would equivalently annihilate the decision. Instead, do it blindly. Suppose you decide to arise at the first sound of the alarm clock. On hearing it, never stop to argue the matter. Do not stop to think whether or not you are still tired or whether it is still early. But immediately jump out of bed.

If the execution costs you some trouble or is repugnant to your instincts, as in making a necessary apology, in the time intervening between decision and execution do not even think about what you are going to do. For then the instinctive objections would reappear. At most, think only of the good consequences which your understanding foresees.

If your decision is to avoid an action to which you are attracted by instinct (some licit pleasure, for instance), it will be better not to think of it at all. Every idea tends toward the act. If perchance you *must* think of it, then let it not be a concrete idea. An idea is more compelling the more concrete it is and the stronger impression it makes on you. Consider only the repulsive aspect of the act and its occasions, or its harmful consequences.

This is a means to perform easily acts which are subjectively heroic. Decide upon the act in the light and warmth of some principal motive. Then for the interval preceding its execution do not think about the act or the contrary motives which unconscious repugnance will present. In short, *you should not think about an act for a longer time than you need to reach a decision.* And when the moment comes, execute it blindly as if it were something automatic which it were impossible not to do.

To make the most effective use of the will, the queen of our faculties, we should accustom ourselves to follow this procedure. On feeling an impulse to do this or that, we should always leave an interval between it and carrying out the impulse. This is allowing time for deliberation. It is the same as saying, "Look before you leap." Before the act of will itself we should ask ourselves, "Shall I actually will this [something concrete]? For what motives?" In the decision itself we should answer, "I do really will it," or "It will be done." We make a firm and concrete act of the will and buttress it by feeling its possibility, usefulness and even necessity. Then we should finally clinch the matter by excluding even the thought of an opposite decision, insisting with ourselves, "It's all settled. Now we go into action."

OUTLINE DIAGRAM

✦

Re-Education of the Will

Definition — { tendency toward the good / our executive power / energy that is free, active, guided by intelligence

Will acts —
- *false* will acts — { mere desire / vague intention / instinctive impulse / velleity ("I would like to")
- aspects of *true* will acts — mental — { concrete object / possibility felt to be so / motive / sincere decision

Re-education — { feel your act of will / progress from external to internal acts / decide the means to take

Execution —
- immediate
- long-term — { do not discuss the plan decided / do not even think about it till the time comes

V

Feelings and Emotions

Although intellectual error brings many to the precipice of evil and disgrace, wanton feelings and emotions are responsible for many more physical tragedies.

EXTERNAL AND INTERNAL sense experiences affect the sensible part of our organism. Merely speculative ideas or images affect the understanding; decisions affect the will. Many of these are only partial reactions of our human system and pass, without other consequences, into the archives of our memory. But there are certain other experiences, ideas and memories with an affective charge of fear or hope, joy or sadness, hatred, wrath, love, etc.; and these affect our whole being. They do not pass away so readily. Their residue tends to become encrusted in our body and keeps influencing the higher levels of personality. Certain feelings and emotions resonate in our nervous system and our whole being, in one way at the presence of happiness, in another way at its absence. Real or imaginary success, for instance, is accompanied by positive emotions. Negative emotions accompany failure or disgrace.

Pleasant feelings help to preserve our normal physiological rhythms. But in emergency situations emotions arise which modify these rhythms, activate our muscular system, and stimulate hormonal production. This total resonance—in the activation of our nervous, muscular and hormonal systems—is necessary for normal development and the balanced functioning of our organism and our spirit. So, for instance, if a child grows up without enough love, security and joy, he will become defective or abnormal. When there is an emotional deficiency in childhood, often the youth or adult turns out to be a social misfit, even as infant malnutrition is related to later proclivity to tuberculosis. The emotionally starved child in some cases later turns out to have a cold and calculating temperament, incapable of affection. Another will have an exaggerated tendency to hatred, suspicion and sadness. Another will be timid, self-belittling, indecisive or a frustrated pessimist. As the remedy for malnutrition is a fortified diet, so the remedy for emotional starvation includes a prolonged injection of positive emotions.

On the other hand, excessively prolonged or intensified *negative* emotions, such as wrath, fear and sadness, can leave the spirit and body of a man conditioned or inclined toward disgust, insecurity and frustration. And this is especially true when he has not been prepared in childhood for the struggles of life.

There is an intricate labyrinth of definitions and theories about feelings or emotions, their species, causes and effects. But the main point of interest in a practical manual such as this is to know their influence on mental fatigue, weakness and psychosomatic diseases, and to point out some norms for channeling and governing them.

EMOTIONAL MACHINERY: THE PSYCHO-PHYSIOLOGICAL TRAJECTORY OF AN EMOTION

Any event may be the occasion of emotions: the sight of a lightning bolt or a savage animal, a lion's roar or the crash of thunder, insults from an enemy, the death of a dear one, a sudden pain, news that surgery is needed, business or academic failure, or even a vivid memory of a great past danger or humiliation.

By the pathways of the senses or imagination these stimuli reach the cerebral cortex. Then my reason, if I am alert, will analyze and interpret them peacefully, and relate them to my happiness without giving room to a frantic imagination to go to work on them. But if I perceive, or think I perceive, in them something contrary to my happiness—or the symbols of happiness such as life, health, comfort, wealth, honor, personal caprice, or my ideals—then my cerebral cortex will send to the hypothalamus, down in my middle brain, an alarm or emergency call asking for the tremendous force of the emotions to be released for defense of my happiness. And emotional force is unleashed on the instant.

The *occasion* of our wrath or fear is the event. But the real cause is in the "Ego," in the interpretation we give to the event, using either our reason or imagination, and connecting the event with our own personal happiness. If we see in the event

EMOTIONAL MACHINERY

an obstacle which we must remove or destroy, we react by anger. If we see it as a danger or mighty opposing force which we cannot overcome, our reaction is fear. If the event means our own failure or some loss, we grow sad. The emotion itself is produced, consciously or unconsciously, by an idea or mental image. In brief, an angry reaction may be summarized in these key words: "*I, He, It.*" "I who am so good, so wise . . . I cannot tolerate such treatment. My status and wishes should be respected." Or, "He or They . . . are unjust, cruel, discourteous . . . and should be reprimanded." Or, "It (the event) is intolerable." In fear, the content of the emotion will be, for instance, "A great harm or danger is hovering over me; it is unavoidable." And in sadness and depression, "My loss is total and irreparable."

Organic effects.—Any of these thoughts, or a memory or vivid image of them is like an alarm signal which goes to the hypothalamus in the middle brain to summon our emotional energy to protect our happiness. The hypothalamus is, as it were, the "control room" of our emotional machinery. It responds instantaneously, sets up the vegetative nervous system for struggle, immediately tenses the muscles (a battle attitude), and, if the emotion is intense, also puts our internal secretion glands into a state of hyperactivity. Such tension, if intense or repeated, may affect the whole organism or its weakest parts and produce functional disorders and pains which are called psychosomatic: somatic because they affect the body (soma); psychical because they are produced by ideas and feelings in the psyche (in the "spirit").

If the tension is localized in the blood vessels, we grow pale because they contract (as in fear). Other emotions dilate the blood vessels and then the skin flushes and turns red. It is thought that 80 per cent of headaches are caused by the narrowing of the medium-sized blood vessels which penetrate into the brain. Anxiety to see better or to read faster produces tension in the eye's accommodation muscles, and so a great many functional visual defects. Tension in the larynx causes 95 per cent of hysterical "lumps in the throat" and consequent trouble with swallowing and breathing. Pains in the nape of the neck are, in 75 per cent of cases, caused by tension in the neck muscles.

When tension is connected with the lungs, we experience a feeling of suffocation or hyperventilation, and even dizziness or nausea, for we are then losing carbon dioxide and not getting enough oxygen. Regarding the heart, most instances of taquicardia, or strong palpitations, have an emotional source.

After the heart and lungs the digestive tract is most frequently affected by the emotions. A study made at Massachusetts General Hospital showed the following: 96 per cent of the colitis cases were nourishing feelings of resentment; 75 per cent suffered from feelings of discouragement; 68 per cent were being tortured by remorse. The bitter wave of hatred or sadness was overflowing into their intestines. Half of the diabetic and cardiopathic cases examined were influenced by emotions either causing or accompanying them. And many cases of arterial hypertension, with no trace of an organic cause, were improved by improving the patient's mental attitudes.

Bad news or a bad mood often result in loss of

appetite, indigestion or nausea. Such renowned institutions as the Mayo Clinic and the Oschner Clinic attribute 74 to 75 per cent of their gastro-intestinal cases to an emotional origin.

Seventy per cent of cases of constipation are attributed to sadness or disgust, and many cases of diarrhea are due to fear or anxiety. Just one case in point: that of the widow who suffered from severe constipation while her two sons were away from home at a boarding school, but was perfectly normal whenever her boys were living at home.

Prolonged tension can produce pain: an ulcer-like pain in the stomach, an appendicitis-like pain in the upper colon, other pains in the lower colon. Fifty per cent of these cases are found to have an emotional cause.

None of all this means that such pains or troubles are unreal or purely due to the patient's imagination. They are real, physical illnesses. A doctor will examine the patient and perhaps make a diagnosis that there is nothing wrong. This means that the organs are completely healthy, but their functioning is disturbed by some emotion. Such a functional illness, if uncorrected, can in the progress of time affect the organ itself.

Repeated tension related to the skin causes many cases of neurodermatitis, and in the limbs muscular rheumatism or fibrositis. And the richer our affective endowment and clearer our intelligence, the more exposed we are to such illnesses if we do not control ourselves. For we shall be able to see a dozen points worth our active concern where those less endowed would see only one, and we shall also be inclined to take upon ourselves many more responsibilities.

We may call this whole process the spontaneous and simple muscular phase of an emotion. It develops within fractions of a second without time for deliberation, and so there can be in it no question of moral responsibility or sin. We call this phase "muscular" because its effects can be explained by muscular reaction without much hormonal intervention. We call it "simple" to distinguish it from other kinds of excitation which are stronger and which at once summon into action the full force of hormonal activity.

The More Conscious and Active Emotion ("hormonal phase")

In this phase, organic commotion reaches and affects the cerebral cortex. We become aware that our muscles are preparing for attack or defense. Sometimes the stimulus itself, or the memory of it, persists. There may be, then, three reactions: from the reason, the imagination, or the will.

1. We may allow our *reason* to think peacefully about the event and the accompanying bodily commotion. On discovering that the latter is really unnecessary and the event not really disastrous and that it may involve other good and greater effects, the disturbance settles down and peace returns. But too often, unfortunately, we give rein to the imagination instead.

2. The imagination peremptorily demands that *full attention* be given to its fears, disgust or sadness. It is then very difficult to concentrate on anything else whatsoever. Recall, for instance, what happens in a moment of wrath. If anyone comes to speak to us about another matter, we can scarcely pay attention to what he is saying. The same thing happens if we are seriously worried. Then it is very difficult to pay attention to the content of a lecture or conference. The emotional force demands that full attention be paid to itself. And such full attention easily terminates in a complete blocking of the mind in one of the following forms:

a) *An obsession.*—A sexual thought or a thought of a present or imminent disaster will not leave us in peace for a moment, unless we busy ourselves with something extremely interesting. It struggles continually to occupy the center of our attention. A scruple is no more than an obsession of fear. The way to conquer it is by giving less importance to the imaginary eternal loss, convincing ourselves that it is an emotional illness which cannot have eternal consequences and by diverting our attention from the thought which produces the emotion. So we shall refuse to follow that train of thought even for the sake of removing the doubt, in practice treating the thought with disdain.

b) *A fixation.*—Unpleasant impressions or thoughts tend to *engrave themselves and become* fixed in our minds by repetition unless we succeed in forgetting or ignoring them. They will be engraved even deeper if we give them importance and fear them. A case in point would be that of the person who struggles against impure thoughts in a spirit of fear. They would gradually disappear if he despised them (instead of fearing them) and, in practice, went on as if he did not have them. Worry is a fine thread of fear which traces a path across the life of our spirit. Unless we succeed in breaking it early, while it is still weak, it will open up into a deep crevasse into which all our attention and thoughts will be channeled.

c) *Exaggeration.*—The ills or dangers that beset us will almost always tend to be exaggerated. If we surrender to this tendency to exaggerate, we shall end up terrified or infuriated by trivialities. If we have caught ourselves in this type of exaggeration, we should learn a lesson to apply to our whole life: "I see that I have a personal one, and that a small one. Therefore, whenever I catch myself worrying a lot in advance, I shall react with a deliberately chosen attitude of joy and smiling peace, because I know that the reason for fear is insignificant."

d) *Transfer.*—Finally we can transfer the emotion from its true cause to one of its concomitant circumstances, as in the case of conditioned reflexes. Take, for example, the case of a child who was hurt and frightened at receiving an injection from a nurse dressed in white, and afterwards was frightened by anything colored white. How important for him to discover early the cause of this false transference!

By interpreting the stimulus, the imagination can strengthen and repeat the negative feelings of sadness or fear. And such a repetition is, as we hinted earlier, the principal cause of very many psychosomatic illnesses. Such an illness can at times be incurred by a single, very strong experience, a psychical trauma. One man, for instance, started across the railroad tracks without noticing that an electric train was coming. The train passed so close to him that it almost grazed him. His emotional reaction was so strong that he fainted dead away before he took a dozen steps further. At the hospital they found so much sugar in his blood that they treated him as a diabetic. But when he regained consciousness, he assured them he had never been a diabetic, and told them the story of what happened.

Most frequently such emotional illnesses come about as the result of *minor* emotions which are, however, repeated often. The following case will be an illustration from animal psychology. Electric wires are attached to the feet of sheep and, while they are grazing peacefully, enough current is sent through for them to feel it. The animals tremble for a moment, the current is interrupted, and they go on feeding in peace. Every five minutes this experience is repeated, for weeks on end, without their organisms becoming in the least abnormal. Then an emotional element is introduced into the experience. A bell is rung ten seconds before the current is turned on. The sheep soon relate the sound of the bell with the unpleasantness of the electric shock. As soon as they hear the bell, they stop grazing and go into a state of painful anticipation. When this experience is repeated every five minutes for several days, the animals stop eating altogether, will not even stand up on their feet, and finally go into a labored breathing which signals death. And so the experiment had to be stopped.

How much emotional rest does an organism need in order to keep off death? Or how long a time should pleasant emotions last in order to counter the effect of unpleasant emotions?

When the sheep were given two to four hours of pleasant experiences as a daily rest, they resisted perfectly the impact of the unpleasant emotions for the rest of the day. This is not unlike the case of human beings. If we make of family life a haven of love, the negative emotions we may experience in office or factory will be counteracted. If we have a sincere spiritual life, in it we shall find the best counterweight to daily dissatisfactions and fears. If in prayer we take account of the fact that we are having an interview with Infinite Wisdom, Goodness and Power, this will give us a great degree of satisfaction. And if, in the performance of our duties, we understand that we are fulfilling the will of God—that is, the ideal of Infinite Wisdom or, in other words, that we are doing the noblest and most useful task that anyone could accomplish in the circumstances—we can have hours of emotional fullness to immunize us against many psychosomatic illnesses.

The third effect of an emotional exaggeration upon our imagination is oftentimes to leave engraved in the subconscious a *permanent feeling or tendency*. So much so that the dividing line tends to disappear between a repeated feeling and a permanent tendency to insecurity, sadness or disgust. The victim of such a tendency feels happy as long as he is kept busy. But as soon as his mind is unoccupied, thoughts of insecurity and sadness enter in, and these rob him of all peace and satisfaction.

The formation of such a tendency, e.g., of insecurity, is not due so much to the actual terror or failure as *a negative manner of reacting to it*. After the event there would be nothing or almost nothing remaining behind in the subconscious if only one were convinced, either by his own efforts or those of his educators or advisers, that there was no such great reason for fear. But if these startling experiences are not balanced by more mature thought, a kind of sediment of insecurity will remain behind after they have passed. And this insecurity will be all the greater depending upon the intensity and frequency of acts, feelings or imagination of terror produced by horror movies, for instance, or horror stories told to children at night time. Such a tendency, mixed with exaggeration, or transference, can produce a lasting disequilibrium, a neurosis. This, as a kind of intruder sun, will disturb one's whole psychical system.

Neurosis—Our internal world may be compared to a planetary system. Around the will, or rational power of appetite, the queen of our faculties, there should gravitate all our psychical life: our sensations, impressions, ideas, reasoning, and deliberate will acts. As in a planetary system, when the sun exerts its influence upon the planets, order reigns and equilibrum, so also in ourselves, when the whole life of our spirit, our psychical life, is obedient to our will. However, if an intruder sun were to insert itself within the orbit of solar attraction and, instead of being subject to the sun, were instead to exercise its own attraction upon the other stars or planets, there would arise disequilibrium and disorder in proportion as it remained independent of the sun and as its own powers of attraction were more intense.

In our interior world this intruder sun would be the strong emotion, not countered or transferred, which takes over within us. Sometimes this would be due to phobia or groundless fear which we cannot master, or a scruple or worry which pursues us incessantly, or a seemingly irresistible attraction or impulse. Such phenomena keep on attracting to themselves other thoughts, acts, feelings. The longer they last, the more satellites they will have, and the weaker and more disturbed will be the will's field of action. To weaken their influence we must remove their satellites. That is, we should not think or act deliberately while under their influence. Most of all, we should find out how they first appeared on the scene within us and how to destroy them.

3. *The third reaction* possible is for the free will to accept the imagination's interpretation of the stimulus, and even assist it by ordering one's actions accordingly. Like the scrupulous person who keeps confessing the same thing over and over again, despite having been forbidden to do so by his director. Or like the man who consents to hatred and attacks his enemy.

With such frequent and so intense irrational reactions in the cerebral cortex, the new stimulation of the hypothalamus will be all the stronger. And if this, at the first signal of alarm, already responds by putting the entire autonomous nervous system in a state of struggle for its own happiness, now it will also throw into action the immense force of the internal secretion glands. The alarm is passed on to the neighboring pituitary gland which directly or indirectly controls the organism's internal hormonal functions. The pituitary gland produces or controls the distribution of a dozen important hormones. Here we are particularly interested in two of them: the adrenocorticotropic hormone (ACTH) and the somatotropic hormone (STH).

Depressive emotions and STH.—When destructive external agents such as poison, infection, heat or cold, invade the organism, the pituitary gland liberates a great quantity of STH to prepare the organism against the invader by providing antibodies, heat, inflammation, etc. The same thing happens when we run into depressing situations or emotions such as sadness, frustration, despair, discouragement, indecision. This excess of STH can produce hypertension, arthritis, asthma, fatigue, and so on. At the Catholic University of Montreal, Dr. Selye kept injecting STH into animals for a period of time and then submitting them to large dosages of salt; he produced hypertension in them. When, instead of giving them salt, he applied cold and moisture to their joints, rheumatoid arthritis appeared. On the other hand, they contracted asthma when he made them inhale a light irritant into their bronchial tubes.

As regards fatigue, we have all had the experience that we tire very soon if we work with an attitude of discouragement, sadness or reluctance or, what comes to the same thing, with an excess of STH. On the other hand, we scarcely feel fatigue when we have enthusiasm, joy and optimism. For instance, a mother feels little fatigue when she is working and watching her beloved child.

Aggressive emotions and ACTH.—At times our emotions are not the kind that wear us down or depress us, but rather aggressive emotions, such as wrath or resentment. Or we fall into the attitude of the eternal reformer, discontent with everything and everybody. Or the idealist or perfectionist who sets a goal beyond his real possibilities and lives in a state of urgency, haste and dissatisfaction; or the overly ambitious person who is driven to overactivity by an uncontrolled sense of competition.

In such instances the pituitary gland liberates the hormone ACTH which does not spread throughout the whole body like STH, but goes to the cortex of the suprarenal glands (above the kidneys) and stimulates them into activity. Here is the principal factory of the hormones which are organic "bombs." They are tiny molecules, but have a great effect on our health or sickness. In the external part of the suprarenal glands, twenty-seven important hormones are produced, among them the well-known cortisone. In the medulla (the internal part) of the suprarenal glands adrenalin is produced. This is a hormone which swiftly gives the organism a great amount of energy for fleeing danger or reaching out to attain happiness. The daily newspapers often supply us with such examples as that of the young mother, a slightly built woman, who was able all by herself to lift the rear end of a heavy automobile from her child. In ordinary circumstances she would have been completely unable to summon such an output of energy.

Here we must needs admire the wisdom of the Creator who arranged that adrenalin would not be produced in the cortex or as an effect of ACTH like the twenty-seven other hormones, for then its saving action would be likely to take effect when it was too late. In such a case (1) the hypothalamus would have to get the alarm signal. Then (2) this would stimulate the pituitary gland. This would then (3) have to liberate ACTH into the bloodstream. (4) Little by little the blood would carry ACTH to the suprarenal glands. And (5) only then would adrenalin be spread throughout the organism to produce the force and strength required. In such a case, we would not have the extraordinary emergency strength which would be needed at a precise emotional moment and would be unable to flee or attack effectively.

But God has so arranged it that adrenalin will not arrive too late. Adrenalin is elaborated in the medulla of the suprarenal glands which is directly connected with the hypothalamus by means of the nervous system. As a result, when the hypothalamus receives the alarm signal, adrenalin is released within fractions of a second.

If these twenty-eight activation hormones are present in excessive amounts as a result of repeated or exaggerated emotions, it is evident that they will disturb its workings and bring on illnesses. Among other distressing effects, they help to produce ulcers, diabetes, hypertension, insomnia, and make us more liable to infection. All this has been demonstrated by Dr. Selye. There follows a summary of some of his experiments.

First, Dr. Selye found that by injecting ACTH, subjecting them to irritating noises, he produced ulcers in rats. Then, to demonstrate emotional malnutrition in man, he conducted a series of experiments at the University of Montreal. He took two groups of children, one group enjoying a happy family life, the other group living in unhappy or broken homes. He saw to it that both groups had the best diet, and frequently examined the functioning of their pituitary glands. He always found an excess of ACTH present in the children who lived in families characterized by terrorism, anger and disgust. Despite their excellent diet, none of these children came up to the normal weight. On the other hand, the children leading a happy family life gained weight and enjoyed robust health.

Our pulse rate at moments of excitement or anger is found to be 170 to 200 or more beats per minute. The blood pressure rises correspondingly from 13 to 23 centimeters or more. A heart attack or a stroke is then possible, and daily experience teaches us that many people with weak hearts or circulatory systems die from these attacks when they are undergoing a period of strong emotions.

We shall consider emotionally caused insomnia and its remedy in the chapter on "Rest" (Ch. VII).

Note, again, that all these illnesses are real and not a fiction of the sick person's imagination, even when the illnesses are induced or increased by the emotions. And we should also note that the richer a man's intellectual life and the nobler and readier his fellow-feelings, the greater probability there may be that he will fall into such illnesses. For the higher our aspirations and the keener our intelligence, the more difficulties we can see and the more distressed we may tend to be in comparison to others less gifted.

CONTROL OF THE EMOTIONS

To control the emotions and avoid such illnesses and unhappiness we propose the following five means:

1) Do not give room to the thought which causes the emotion. Instead, occupy your mind with another matter.

2) By education (or self-education) change your evaluation of the stimulus and become accustomed to consider the stimulus from another viewpoint.

3) Discover and modify the disturbing idea.

4) Change the negative feeling and tendency.
5) Change the expression of it to the extent that it is under your control.

1) Do Not Give Room to the Disturbing Idea.

A) *By avoiding the occasion* of it, you can more easily avoid the thought itself which is aroused on such and such an occasion. This course of action is often possible. And in some matters it is necessary and obligatory; for instance, in cases of sexual excitation. Moral theologians teach us that even to put oneself in such an occasion without necessity is sinful and presumptuous. Since this is such a slippery terrain, if we so much as enter upon it we are liable to fall.

B) *Occupy your whole attention with other matters.*

(1) *By fully conscious sensations* (Ch. III). Recall the case of the young man with a compulsive tendency to suicide. He gained control and was cured by interposing conscious sensations whenever he experienced that impulse.

(2) *Avoid the thought which arouses the emotion by busying yourself with attractive occupations or pastimes.* Have a hobby or harmless amusement to resort to in moments of depression, fatigue or a negative emotion. The smoker who savors a warm puff finds a channel for his emotions. So does the collector who loses himself for a while in his collections. Or the artist with his music or painting, and the gardener with his flowers.

(3) *Pay better attention to what you are doing or saying* rather than to the subjective thoughts which

disturb you; for instance, if you blush or tremble before a public appearance. That is how I myself conquered a childhood fear of cemeteries at night. I deliberately went there alone and spent some time praying for the repose of the souls of those who were buried there. The devotional attitude took up my attention, and so my fearful imagination could not control my mind.

And is not this the way that mothers everywhere handle the emotions of their babies? When the infant cries in fear, anger or sadness, the mother shows it something new and, by distracting its attention, succeeds in interrupting or allaying the childish emotion.

2) Change Your Evaluation of the Stimulus.

The stimulus is connected with a sorrow, humiliation, failure, offense, and so forth. Your course of action is to weigh carefully just what good elements there are in such an event. Then you will have pleasant thoughts instead of those which are sad, depressing or frustrating. And if these cross our minds we can control them by the opposite, pleasant thoughts. This is not the work of a day, but the result of an education in magnanimity, goodness, understanding, faith and fortitude. Some of the ancient philosophers of Greece and Rome attained this to a high degree guided only by the light of natural reason. They insisted that we must accept suffering as a help to be stronger and more understanding and patient with others.

However, in the most difficult and bitter crises of life it is scarcely possible for merely philosophical considerations to bring us equanimity and joy. For sorrow, humiliation, failure, sickness and death seem meaningless when we separate them from considerations of God and eternity. At such moments only religion offers us a peaceful point of view. Then if we look upon ourselves as pilgrims in this world, moving in the direction of our eternally happy homeland, it is possible to depreciate a passing sorrow. And if we meditate upon what Holy Scripture says about a passing tribulation producing for us "an eternal weight of glory," we can even begin to rejoice at suffering.

A deeply religious education makes such a solution easier. Such an educational background will include as a model an Infinite God who deliberately chose suffering and humiliation for Himself, for His Mother and His Apostles. Only in the light of eternity can we make light of temporal afflictions. And we can accept human suffering and humiliations in the light of the divine honor and joy which we expect to receive in return for them. We can come to love such sufferings or humiliations only if we imitate the saints and look upon them as the caresses, embraces, love and mercy of our Heavenly Father and signs of divine predilection.

In the chapters of Part II we shall explain the concrete methods by which we can overcome thoughts which cause wrath, fear and sadness.

3) Discover and Change the Disturbing Idea.

Modify: a) its content; b) the reason for it; c) its intensity and duration.

a) *Modify its content.*—When the cause is conscious and concrete, it is easy to discover where it is exaggerated or illogical, and so it is easier to modify it. But sometimes we unconsciously suppress it because we do not wish inadmissible acts or motives to appear even in our minds. At other times we transfer it to other stimuli or concomitant causes. In such instances consultation with a specialist is indicated. A subconscious anxiety or disturbance in your feelings can be normalized or diminished when the idea producing it is made conscious. Hence it follows that many emotional conflicts are cured once they are made manifest and examined minutely. A detailed examination of the content of feelings and their causes and discovering the conditioned reflex in many phobias or the transference which produced them can often weaken or even do away with them. The account of conscience or report to one's personal spiritual director—practiced by many persons who are serious about progress in their spiritual life—often produces the same beneficial result.

b) *Modify the reason for it.*—The reason for a feeling which may now seem illogical but which, nevertheless, we cannot now control can often be made clear if we rediscover some forgotten circumstance or repressed tendency originally associated with it. Psychiatric evaluation or certain psychological tests (the T.A.T., for instance) can help discover it and set one free of its harmful effects.

A case in point: J. B. experienced a feeling of asphyxiation or difficulty in breathing whenever he entered a theater or a church and, to avoid this, always had to sit near a door. Was this feeling linked up with an idea of being shut in? He did not know. But when he was helped to recall the first time that

he experienced this, a serious illness that befell him
in a closed room, he experienced lasting relief.

c) The intensity or emotional force of an idea
depends upon three factors.

(1) *Its quality.*—The more concretely an idea is
represented, the more immediate force it has. The
more spiritual or abstract it is, the less emotional, but
more enduring, motive force. That is why orators
speak to the imagination to obtain an immediate
result, a feeling. But when they want a lasting
effect, they try to convince the understanding.

(2) *Its quantity.*—The force of an idea is greater
in proportion to its closer association with other
ideas, experiences or feelings, and to the degree to
which they are more striking.

(3) *Its duration.*—A passing emotion, fear or sadness leaves little trace in the organism or mental
background. But if it remains too long it can modify
them to a notable extent. It can attract into its orbit
(as we said of the intruder sun) more and more
thoughts and acts, and cause lasting disorder.

In several parts of South America I witnessed the
following custom, a very pious one, if you will, but
not very Christian. And it is by no means in accordance with mental hygiene. Women there will remain
in mourning for months and months without going
out of the house or admitting any distractions. When
the period of mourning is over, many of them have
become nervous cases. Because it persisted, the
depressing atmosphere of mourning destroyed their
control.

Take the idea then that is bothering you and strip
it of its sensible counterpart, its importance and con-

crete details. Break the links it has with other phenomena of your experience. Do not consciously
dwell on it, but, as mentioned heretofore, substitute
for it a contrary thought and feeling or at least a
different one. In making this substitution, search for
other ideas which appeal to the senses as much as
possible. Symbols will have a strong appeal to your
(or the patient's) imagination. Associate these ideas
with important living realities. Repeatedly pass
them through your mental field of consciousness
that, like a snowball, they may gather round them
as large a number of mental elements as possible.

4) Change the Negative Feeling and Tendency to the Opposite.

Sometimes we do succeed in changing *the idea*,
but still experience an inclination toward the scruple,
worry, sadness, discontent, or fear. This means that
the negative *feeling* is still rooted in the subconscious and tends to bother the mind with negative
thoughts. If we do not keep our mind well occupied,
we shall find it possessed by sad memories, worries,
disgust and fears which are allied to that latent
feeling or tendency.

The indirect remedy consists in giving no room to
these thoughts, always keeping the mind busy until
the tendency to sadness or fear atrophies from
disuse.

The direct remedy is to change the latent tendency or, better, to implant the opposite one.
Understanding how such a tendency is formed will
instruct us how to fight this battle. The tendency
to fear, for instance, as we have indicated above,
comes about as a consequence of vivid experiences

of fear which are not countered by vivid experiences of security. So, then, a moment of terror, or repeated feelings of fear, or thoughts and feelings of insecurity tend to remain within us as a kind of sediment which inclines us to a fear mentality. But if these negative impressions have been swiftly opposed by other thoughts and positive feelings, they leave scarcely any trace within us. Note, for instance, how a frightened child is comforted by his parents or teachers. And an adult manner of dealing with a sudden fright, disgust or failure is to reason about it and to conclude that it was not so terrible after all.

A contrary example. A little four-year-old girl, playing with a puppy, did not notice a huge dog jump over the fence, but heard it hit the ground just behind her. She was terrified, screamed, wept, ran away and could never be near any dog without trembling with terror. I knew her years later when she was a doctor running a clinic in a capital city of the Far East. She admitted to me that the phobia was still with her and so overcame her once in a Paris restaurant that, when a man brought a dog into the restaurant, she lost control of herself and climbed up on the table out of its reach. If her mother had only done with her what another mother, better prepared for such an incident, did with her little girl! The very next day, while her little girl was eating near a door which opened onto their garden, the mother came into view at a distance leading a dog on a leash. When the little girl started to become frightened and screamed, her mother said, "Don't be afraid. This is a very good dog, and I have him on the leash." Then the little girl quieted down and went on with her dinner. Every day her mother brought the dog a little nearer, with a similar outburst of fright from the little girl, then victory over it. After about thirty such positive experiences the little girl was cured of her phobia.

Whenever the tendency stays rooted in the subconscious, it must not be allowed to grow. The opposite feelings must be implanted. The tendency will not increase if we do not continue to feed it with negative thoughts, conversations, actions and attitudes. We shall control and eliminate it if we act out the contrary, positive emotional situations. A single very strong positive feeling can sometimes be a complete cure of such a tendency.

In his youth, despite a strong and attractive personality, Francis de Sales was almost overcome by a scruple of conscience. One day, in a state bordering on despair despite repeated confessions, he went into a church and spoke to Our Lord: "If I am to hate and curse you throughout all eternity in hell, at least I want to love and praise you now in this life with all my strength." And for a good long time he gave a free rein to sentiments, previously repressed, of love of God. He walked out of that church cured of his scruple forever. This strong feeling and positive emotion of love had destroyed the negative attitude of fear and insecurity which had been causing his scrupulosity.

So, in handling these difficulties, we must especially be sure to implant the opposite feeling and tendency. Love and sympathy counteract antipathy and hatred, as we shall explain in the chapter on anger. Against insecurity and fear we should use heroic decisions, acts which embrace positive values and trains of thought which imply security. Against sadness we should repeat ideas and attitudes which are joyful. When the new, positive "sediment" produced by a positive manner of thinking and acting equals or is greater than the negative tendency which has accumulated in our interior life, then we shall be cured. If the cure is not complete, at least we shall experience definite relief.

5) Change the External Expression of the Feeling.

The emotion has a fulcrum in its physiological counterpart, i.e., the external expression of eyes, breathing, voice, and muscles. If you remove this support and, even better, "act out" the opposite external expression as far as possible, you weaken or extinguish the undesirable feeling.

In fear or anger the eyes become hard, staring, and blink scarcely at all. The road to victory in moments of irritation is to relax the eyes deliberately, blink often, and try to smile with the eyes. The day after I explained this to a group of college students, one of them came to me and said with enthusiasm: "Father, this is terrific. Last night I was about to lose my temper, but I remembered what you said in your talk. I relaxed my eyes and smiled with them; I took a few deep breaths and controlled myself so well that my mother, who was listening in the next room, came in afterwards to congratulate me and ask me to explain to her how I did it."

In a state of emotion the voice tends to be hard and trembling. So, in a moment of wrath, you should keep quiet or answer very softly. Speak in a stronger tone of confidence when you feel fear, and in moments of sadness use a more animated tone of voice. Popular wisdom tells us all this in the proverbs of many languages. In English, the expression "To whistle in the dark" expresses a method of conquering fear. Songs are a proverbial cure for sadness even as far back as the words of St. James' Epistle. The Japanese have a more poetical expression: "When the face smiles, the sun comes out in the heart." We should, then, relax and soften the lines of facial expression and unclench tense hands in emotional moments.

All by itself this physiological control of an emotion, acting out the opposite expression of it, will often not be enough. In certain cases it may even be harmful, if we continue to hold on to the exciting thought. But if we add to physiological control the management of our spirit, by arousing contrary thoughts and feelings, victory will be swift and sure.

Putting together these two means last mentioned (contrary feelings and expressions), we come to a practical technique for overcoming deep-rooted feelings. We must live out in our imagination the circumstances that have so great an effect on us, then describe with a *tone* of conviction the emotional state in which we should be, or would like to be, or in which normal persons would be. This *tone* of security, if it is intense, will produce a proportionate *feeling* to counteract the phobia.

Father Laburu tells the story about a country boy who was terrified of locusts. Whenever he saw one close by, he began to tremble, lose his wits, and run. In his case this was practically uncontrollable and he would have even thrown himself out the window if he found no other way to get out of the room. Father Laburu told him to *imagine* that a locust was flying through the door and then had him say, "I am perfectly calm," imitating a tone of security. "The locust is getting nearer," said the psychologist, and the boy repeated this after him. Imagining a locust coming closer, the boy began to be frightened. But by keeping on saying, "And I am perfectly calm; it makes no difference to me," he did grow calm. Then Father Laburu had him say, "The locust is right next to me. It is in Father's hands" (Father Laburu had brought one in a small jar). "Now it is in my hands" (he had him take in his hands the bottle with the locust); "I am perfectly calm." Scarcely had he uttered this last phrase in a tone of great control when a deep breath of relief and an open smile showed his complete liberation from the phobia. Once the first phase of emotion has been brought under control, we begin to experience the consoling effects of emotional control in body and soul both. These are the following: greater muscular relaxation, a calming down of nervousness, glandular and hormonal equilibrium. Health is preserved and improved. We feel a greater strength and serenity, and a deeper sense of joy. We gain easier victory over our lower instincts. We begin to have a stronger and more balanced personality, to know internal and social peace. Greater happiness is ours, and there is edification of our neighbor. And, finally, we please God more and work for His greater glory.

EXAGGERATED IMPRESSIONABILITY

This exaggeration is a result of the fact that the *organism itself* is weakened, tense, or producing an excessive amount of certain hormones. But this exaggeration depends also, and especially, on the life of our *spirit* and the ideas and patterns of thought which have become habitual.

1. *Organic Weakness:* sick people, children, women, and the elderly are usually more impressionable than a man in robust health.

2. Muscular tension opens up the way to emotion, and this tension is the first thing produced by emotion. Once this tension is present, a very small stimulus will produce emotional effects which increase rapidly. President Franklin D. Roosevelt was said to have kept a couch in his office where he stretched himself out at odd moments several times a day to relax completely for a few minutes. This muscular relaxation gave him greater equanimity and, as a result, he spoke with greater authority and assurance. Chancellor Adenauer of the Federal Republic of Germany, despite his 82 years, was the man responsible for his country's economic recovery. He had a capacity for prodigious activity, equanimity and long hours of work. He owed this to the fact that every day he took two or three short naps which relaxed all his muscles.

3. Excessive hormonal production is characteristic of one who lets himself be dominated frequently by anger, fear or sadness. It also prepares the way for a second phase of emotion in which the glands become habitually overactive. In a word, these are the "stress illnesses" described by Dr. Selye. Whether injected or produced by the organism itself, adrenalin makes us more irritable.

GREATER IMPRESSIONABILITY

This depends especially on the life of our *spirit*, the manner in which we face life. The very same

events have a great effect on some individuals, and
little or no effect on others. Even in the same individual they may have great, small, or no effects,
depending on antecedent circumstances or the element of surprise. Little trace is left behind in persons
whose ideas, convictions or feelings permit them to
see in such events other aspects to counterbalance
the sadness or fear, desire or worry. For instance,
two different men, one avaricious and proud, the
other disinterested and humble, suffer the same
reverse of fortune and go bankrupt. The first will
be very depressed and sad. If he does not know how
to distract himself and face his misfortune in a positive manner, it will eventually dominate him and
bring complete loss of control. The second man,
however, full of positive ideas and feelings, will not
experience so great a shock. When the first reaction
has passed, he will almost instinctively, as it were,
be able to find even happiness in his new situation.

The Root of Exaggerated Impressionability

We must seek for this on the level of our lower
mental activities. These do not perceive higher realities and take us away from the true reality of things,
of life and of our own personality. Exaggerated
impressionability is rooted in the following instincts:
those of self-preservation, domination and reproduc-
tion. There is an innate *tendency to preserve* our
physical, bodily nature by the reaction of flight from
danger and bodily death without bothering about
what is spiritual and eternal. There is also a *tendency to win out over others* and increase our own
earthly goods or reputation without taking into
account whether this impedes other still greater

goods. There is, finally, *a tendency to seek pleasure for one part* of our being even if it be to the detriment of the whole. This is also an impulse to flee from pain and hardship although these may bring higher goods to us. The right to our inheritance is sold for a mess of pottage. Sexual or alcoholic pleasure is sought, even though ruinous to health.

We do not take into account the true reality of man. Man is not only body but spirit also. He is not only earthly and temporal but heavenly and eternal. We do not even take our own personality into account. For we refuse to accept limitations imposed on us by heredity or environment. As a result, the emotional center of gravity is thrown off balance.

This center of gravity in man is the sublime goal given him by the Creator. Man is to dispose of himself according to the good pleasure of the Infinite Being so that afterwards he may enjoy Him for all eternity. Whoever realizes the sublime dignity of being able to fulfill at each moment the ideal God sets for us, that is, "to want what He does and do what He wants," and realizes that this cannot be impeded by sickness or poverty or another's evil or injustice—such a person is less likely to suffer a lasting mental disturbance. The saints understood this sublime goal and lived it, and they are, thus, models of self-control. For this reason, too, believers who suffer emotional disturbances will do very well to add to scientific methods the still more effective method of the *Spiritual Exercises*[1] of St. Ignatius Loyola.

---

[1] A practical manual which outlines considerations and meditations to lead to the reformation and sanctification of one's personal life. These spiritual exercises, continued through several days, are commonly known as a "retreat," or "making a retreat."

By meditating on this great truth in his first exercise, called the *Principle and Foundation*,[2] they will balance their center of gravity again and will feel their fears and worries disappear in the deepest peace of soul.

In Lima, where I received a great deal of real help in missionary propaganda from an active and businesslike lady, I stood in admiration of the serenity which the following thought habitually brought her in spite of contradictions and failures. "In comparison with God, the Infinite Being, all men are like a little grain of sand. And how much less am I? But if this atom can bring a smile to the Infinite Being, why be lost in worry about whether other atoms are praising Him or not? And why lose time thinking merely about myself, my illnesses, virtues or defects?"

Preventive Remedy

Begin at the root cause first. Fix the hierarchy of values firmly in the understanding by a good moral and religious education. Form a correct apprecia-

---

[2] According to St. Ignatius the *Principle and Foundation* of our whole spiritual life reads as follows:

"Man was created to praise, reverence and serve God, Our Lord, and by this means to save his soul. All other things on the face of the earth were created for man, to help him pursue the end for which he was created. Hence it follows that he should use them insofar as they help him toward his end, and should abstain from them insofar as they obstruct him. So as far as it is permitted our free will to do so and is not forbidden, we should make ourselves indifferent to all created things, in this sense that for our part we do not seek for health rather than sickness, riches rather than poverty, honor rather than disgrace, a long life rather than a short one, and similarly in all other matters. We should desire and choose only what better leads us to the end for which we have been created" (*Exercitia Spiritualia*, in *Thesaurus Spiritualis Societatis Iesu*, Bruges, Desclée, 1932, pp. 34–37).

tion of what is lasting and eternal as superior to what is but temporal and passing. Set the total good of your whole being above the partial good of your body alone. Illuminate and direct your instincts toward their right road and goal. Elevate them by knowledge and faith to heights with which they are themselves unacquainted.

You must strive to appreciate and work toward your total good. You must have a self-love which is not creeping, earthly or material but higher, spiritual and eternal. It must be a love of the life and glory which will not end, a love of suffering dignified by the ideal of bearing it as God's will, a disinterested love of others. If you have supernatural Faith and Charity, love your neighbor because in him you see your Creator disguised in his defects. Thus you can love and serve God with greater merit.

You can attain this by meditation on higher goods and practice of the virtues. The more you strengthen your higher mental activities by the understanding of higher values and by positive decisions for good, the more you will be immune from the disorders of lower instincts. In the case of the saints this dominion of reason and right morals reaches its culmination. Disgrace, humiliation and temporal dangers caused them no worries whatsoever.

Secondly, in your conduct avoid any ideas or surroundings, sights or acts which favor distorted tendencies. Block unlawful satisfaction of instinct for this engraves and stamps false values into your very being.

INTEGRAL RELIGIOUS PSYCHOTHERAPY

Considering the remedies indicated in this chapter,

especially if we go to the depths of the problem, we might conclude that atheism, materialism, or a vague deism create a poor psychotherapy which satisfies neither heart nor reason. If we consider only man's physiology and not his spiritual soul with its aspirations toward the infinite, if we separate him from God and do not orient him toward his Maker, Father, and Eternal Happiness, then we disintegrate him psychically and separate him from reality. Then he becomes disjointed. In the most intimate part of his being there will always be a vacuum of existential anguish. The edifice of security, satisfaction, optimism, robust personality, and a realization of limitless values, which we desire to construct upon such a foundation, will have no solidity. Nor can it offer resistance to a sudden reverse of fortune.

On the other hand, a psychotherapy which is founded upon faith and the divine destiny of man calms and satisfies the reason, feelings, the soul itself and the whole nervous system. It keeps a man normal, integral, serene, and sublime even amid the greatest suffering and in the face of death itself. Evidence for this is the thousands of martyrs and saints of every age, race, and condition of life.

At the seventh International Catholic Congress of Psychotherapy held in Madrid, September 1957, a desire was evident to integrate analytic findings with the Catholic concept of man. Such an integration could perhaps be attained more easily if we followed the technique of Dr. Martinez Arango of Havana and the directives of Dr. Caruso, i.e., to consider man in his total reality as a "child of God and heir to heaven." Freud was the discoverer of a "new world" in psychotherapy. He discovered the unconscious forces in man. But since he disregarded what is spiritual and supernatural in us, he gave an excessive importance to the instinctive mechanisms of the "libido." Adler parted ways with Freud when he did not find in the teachings of his master that other great unconscious force, the instinct to "domination." He himself explained and utilized this mechanism of "domination." Jung went even further and caught a glimpse of the supernatural or the divine without, however, formulating it as anything more than an archetype or collective unconscious.[3] If these great visionaries had known that we came from God, that we are sparks from the hearth of Infinite Love, if they had understood that the insatiable thirst for love and happiness which we experience are the urgings of our Heavenly Father to transform ourselves in Him and share in His infinite happiness, perhaps then they would have conceived and explained clearly what they left indefinite, and would have avoided many corrections and contradictions in their theories.

It is logical and understandable that, since man has fallen from the original elevated state in which God placed him, he should experience a certain vital anguish. But redeemed man can easily overcome such an obstacle and see that he is provided with so many means, suffering included, of elevating him-

---

[3] Finally, in 1932, Jung wrote, "During the last 30 years people have consulted me from all civilized regions of the world . . . and among my patients of the last 35 years I have not found a single one whose problem did not ultimately consist in seeking a religious perspective in his life. I can affirm with complete assurance that they had all become ill because of having lost what religion has always offered to its adherents, and that they were cured when they regained their religious perspective."

self to a divine level. For whoever deals with divine wealth can scarcely be overly concerned with earthly affairs of lesser importance. In this manner we can have an easier solution to many cases of frustration, despair, phobia, disgust, conflict, repression, fixation, and worry.

Some Crucial Problems and Their Solution in Psychotherapy

There are some transcendental problems which consciously or unconsciously urge themselves upon every rational being and which can be, in him, the occasions of sadness, despair and pessimism. For instance, the origin and end of the world; who made it and for whom? Who governs it? Why are we here in it? Why do we suffer and die? What happens after death?

In the synoptic table on the two following pages we shall compare the solutions and replies which are given us by atheistic or materialistic psychotherapists and the solutions and effects which religion offers us.

CRUCIAL PROBLEMS AND THEIR SOLUTION IN PSYCHOTHERAPY

Origin and Destiny of the World and Man. Suffering. Death.

Solution

Atheistic and Materialistic Psychotherapy	*Religious Psychotherapy*
Does not know the origin of the world nor why it exists.	The world comes from a wise and perfect Creator to help man toward perfection.
Chance governs it, i.e., no one.	It is governed by God, a loving Father, omnipotent.
We are in it as the most perfect animals, without being able to satisfy our thirst for love, peace, joy and accomplishment.	We are here as on a passageway toward complete happiness: —to increase it by our merits. —to glorify our Infinite Father. After death we shall love and enjoy God.
Suffering is inadmissable; it has no advantage. Death is annihilation, the end of everything.	Suffering perfects us and increases our reward. Death is the end of exile and entrance into our fatherland.

Effects

Does not satisfy reason: it leaves behind intellectual insecurity, doubt about what is most important and transcendental.

Satisfies the reason: with intellectual security and certitude about what is most important for us.

Does not satisfy the heart: it leaves behind a vacuum, anguish, sadness, emotional insecurity.

without an adequate object to love.

without a sufficient feeling of being loved and protected.

without real accomplishment to fulfil the soul's aspirations.

Satisfies the heart: it gives peace, security, confidence, love, joy and full satisfaction.

with an Infinite Goodness to love.

feeling oneself loved and protected by God.

realizing the ideal of Infinite Wisdom.

Consequently:

1. integral psychotherapy needs the spirit of God.
2. a healthy spiritual life is already a superior kind of psychotherapy; it gives us:
   a) *Unity* in our whole life of mind and heart.
   b) *Complete* satisfaction and realization.
   c) *Security* in this life and for eternity.

PSYCHOPHYSIOLOGICAL TRAJECTORY OF FEELINGS

Emotions: an emergency reaction totally disturbing our normal state of happiness.

Occasion: any unusual event or sensation.

Cause: the thought which affects my happiness.

Organic Effects: resulting from muscular tension: a disturbance in digestion, respiration, circulation, and so forth.

Physical Effects:
- Full attention: fixation, obsession, exaggeration, etc.
- Repeated or strong feelings.
- A deeply wrought tendency, e.g., neurosis.

Effects of the Hormonal Phase:
- In depressive emotions: STH, asthma, arthritis, hypertension, fatigue.
- In regressive emotions: ACTH, malnutrition, ulcers, diabetes, infection, insomnia, etc.

Control of These Emotions:
1. Avoid the occasion or the disturbing idea.
2. Change the focal point surrounding the event, and one's own attitude and habits.
3. Discover and modify the idea.
4. Implant the opposite tendency.
5. Assume the opposite expression.
6. Correct the exaggeration in one's impressionability.

Integral Psychotherapy: A comparison of the educational resources of psychotherapy { with religion / without religion

VI

Résumé of Re-Educational Treatment

ONCE CONVINCED that illness or weakness comes from disorders in your mental activities together with alterations in your nervous and muscular system, follow this health decalogue.

I. Begin by learning how to rest. Exercise naturally the easiest of mental acts, *conscious sensations*. This is at once a tonic and sedative. If tension and fatigue are very great, first take a few days rest. Change your environment or occupation, or travel.

II. Then go on to perform perfectly and without tension the second, more active mental act. Concentrate your attention on *a succession* of sensations, images or reasoning processes which you remember from the past or now elaborate in your imagination. Emphasize single-mindedness in your work.

III. In the second or third week, without wholly abandoning the previous exercises, strengthen your will by means of *decisions* that are concrete, progressively more difficult and punctually executed. Sweep out all indecision.

IV. Once your faculties are trained, correct whatever *abnormality* there may be in your feelings. To

this end *first modify the idea or image* which produces them and substitute for it (as soon as it
appears in consciousness) sensations and concentrations which are clearly distinct and, so far as
possible; also pleasant.

V. Then *modify* the emotional overtone of that
idea or feeling which is bothering you. Do this first
by means of reasoning: "This feeling of mine is irrational. Others are not bothered by it; it does not
sadden them as much as it does me. I should react
as others do, as a normal man."

VI. *Associate another, different feeling* with that
idea. Bring the idea consciously to mind and then
imagine other consequences and live out the other
feeling which you will have prepared beforehand.

VII. *Arouse the contrary feeling* in yourself and
make it penetrate even to the subconscious by imagining it vividly and speaking about it with the tone
of voice peculiar to the feeling you wish. And work
as if you already had it. Associate this strong
feeling of security or courage, for instance, with the
idea which formerly produced disturbance or fear.
(Remember the case about the locust.)

VIII. Simultaneously with this whole treatment
repair the expenditure of nervous and muscular
energy which mental tension produces by accustoming your muscles to exercise and due relaxation. Do
this both for the time of waking and sleeping. Waste
no nervous energy in useless movements or tense
postures.

IX. *Avoid the formation of toxins* by eating foods
which are readily digested, and practice regular

elimination. Build up your cells, nerves and muscles through healthy breathing and adequate diet.

X. *Accept the reality* which cannot be modified. Found your ideal upon reality. Fill out your human ideal with sublime truths which are eternal and divine.

APPLICATIONS AND PRACTICAL ADVICE
FOR MALADJUSTMENTS OF PERSONALITY

Know Yourself

Weakness or illness is no mere imagination or fiction. Symptoms felt in head, heart or digestive apparatus are real symptoms. In general, however, they are not caused by a lesion in your organs, but by uncontrolled mental activity or the chaotic subconscious. Consult a specialist, and, if he agrees about the integrity of the organs, there should be no further worry about this decision. You must attend to and convince yourself of the fact that these symptoms owe their origin and intensity to mental causes, or to uncontrolled thought about them and about the illness which seems to afflict them.

The practical conclusion will be not to think of the symptoms or illness voluntarily. Rather practice thinking voluntarily about the clinical decision. Feel your complete health and organic efficiency. To know the mental nature of the illness and to locate the struggle on its true ground will be fifty per cent of the cure. The other fifty per cent is in confidence and faith in the method, together with the time factor.

Think of Others

No one who lives for himself alone lives as fully or produces as much as he who lives for others and does good for others. When you are dominated by your unconscious mental activities, you lead a negative life which is colored by a sickly egoism. You are always thinking of your own troubles and finding ways to lessen them. You can find no time to busy yourself with others or do any positive and progressive work. You see the enemy everywhere and are wholly taken up with fleeing from him.

Such a person lives, as Fosdick puts it, as if in a room lined with mirrors. Wherever he looks he sees himself. But when he busies himself with others, several of these mirrors are changed into windows through which he can see other faces, other lives and other more pleasant landscapes.

You will also find great help in a noble ideal. This may be professional or religious. Let it be some unselfish dedication of your work either out of patriotism, love of your neighbor, or from some religious motive.

I knew a young doctor who was exhausted by his studies and first labors. He was crushed by insomnia, obsessions, fatigue and a sickly egoism. Then he decided to take a trip to rest and distract himself. On his arrival at a Chinese port, a missionary invited him to visit his hospital. He began to interest himself in the illnesses of those good people and lent them his professional services out of compassion. He ended up by remaining as the head of the establishment. He forgot his own ills and was completely cured.

Practice Singleness of Thought

The general cause, remote or proximate, of these mental illnesses is a kind of double thought. Or it is an occupation with several ideas at once (obsessions, fears, worries). Practice singleness of thought, then, in order not to increase your ills.

Imitate St. Bernard, the most active and busiest man of his century. On his shoulders rested the responsibility for his monastery, the composition of admirable books, consultation with princes and even the business of the universal Church. When he entered a church he used to say, "Thoughts of Bernard, remain outside." And he would concentrate on his prayers in peace.

Practice Confidence

To lessen the force of an obsessing idea, a feeling of sadness or worry, you must oppose to it an intimate persuasion that everything in this world passes. Imagined ills are always greater in our minds than they are in reality. Fears of insanity, heart failure or sudden death, which many nervous people have, are never realized. Experience confirms this and doctors attest to it.

Have confidence in your own health and do not be bothered by trivial symptoms of illness. Our organism is so complicated and so exposed to contrary influences that it naturally cannot function for a single day without some friction among its many parts. You may truly say, "This is nothing. It will soon pass away." Remember that however little your attention is worriedly fixed on a sensation, it is thereby disquieted, increased and exaggerated. Conversely, when you shift attention to a different matter, the evil lessens and gradually disappears.

Never did fear or discouragement put off the arrival of threatening evils. What fear or discouragement really does when exaggerated is to dissipate and exhaust the forces and strength you need to go out and resist those evils. If they must come, let them not, by thought, begin to torture you before the time.

Profit by Moderate Discussion

Discuss the matter freely with a prudent and experienced person. Thus you will lessen the discouragement, sadness, worry or fear, and calm the tension. Apart from discussion and consultation with specialists it is better not to speak of your illness or symptoms. The less you think of them, the less they will bother you.

This mental tyranny over you will be softened by freely talking it over with God in prayer if you accept what you have to suffer with great confidence in His love and almighty power.

Suffering is like a perfume. If you open it to human egoism, the fragrance evaporates unperceived. If you open it to God, it rises to Him like incense and comes down to you again like a heavenly dew. "To carry a splinter in one's heart," says Gar-Mar, "and talk of something else is the feat of a hero."

Exercise Conscious Life

When you are not engaged in intellectual work, rest your mind by receiving conscious sensations with an easy, peaceful attention to the things of the external world. And when doing mental work exert yourself in concentrating all your attention there. Forget the past, future and yourself. In the beginning you will do this easily for a few moments. Then by progressive increase of attention you will attain normal concentration.

The root of the evil is in domination of conscious mental activity by the unconscious. Now the acts prescribed above are in themselves insignificant. Yet, because they are fully conscious and often repeated during the day, they attack the root of the evil directly. They produce a reaction of greater joy, peace and mastery.

Don't Be Discouraged

Do not think it strange if in the morning you notice a greater sensation of the symptoms, discouragement or fatigue, and if fatigue is less and sadness almost gone by the afternoon or after doing some work. The reason is that the unconscious is in control during sleep. And there is danger after awakening of continuing under its disturbing influence. After some controlled acts, however, joy returns again and our vigor is rejuvenated.

Nor should you wonder at the periodic appearance of enthusiasm and discouragement, progress and apparent setbacks. This happens in many mental and nervous illnesses.

Fight Pessimism

An uncontrolled imagination drives a man toward pessimism and exaggeration of his troubles, and hence to discouragement and despair. For sad events and experiences, at one time conscious but now perhaps forgotten, continue to be active on the unconscious level. They tend to add a pessimistic overtone to all mental images. If we reflect on our thoughts and feelings we shall see that even insignificant beginnings can have terrifying consequences.

A brief daily examination in writing of the course of your pessimistic imaginings will quickly convince you of this. You will then belittle those fears, troubles and worries. If you discount your fears by 90 per cent, you will be closer to reality. Give no importance then to imagined ills or fears for the future. Better still, once you recognize the error or exaggeration of your unconscious mental associations, deliberately come to the opposite conclusion: enthusiasm, joy, courage, optimism. For, as Father Gar-Mar again said, the shadow of the cross is often larger than the cross itself. So black, so sad, so crushing are the crosses we dream up for ourselves.

Keep Busy

Employ your time well and so distribute it among different tasks that by keeping yourself busy you have no time for worry. To enable the factor of feeling to intervene here, let your undertakings be in the possible and practical order. Make sure they are useful and interesting. Only when the sick imagination finds the field of consciousness unoccupied will it be able to torture you with its sad and discouraging exaggerations. *Idleness and the lack of an ideal produce more neurotics than work ever does.*

A young bride, her mother told me, used to live tormented by fears. One fear was that she would lose her mind. She bore a son, and still the fears continued. In the course of time she had five more children and because she was not rich she had to do all her own housework. Hardly could a worry take shape when a child's wail would bring her flying to its side. Or two of them would start a squabble and she would be off to calm them down. Or she had to get a meal ready, or the ironing board was calling her. Or rain threatened to wet her laundry that was stretched on the line to dry. Some urgent household task would always be taking up her whole attention and coming just in time to kill worries at their first stirring.

The famous Jesuit scholar, Father Wassman, conquered his own depression by taking up the study of ants. In this field he later became so preeminent that the whole world marveled at his books.

Foster Joy and Optimism

Insist upon joy and optimism as opposed to the sadness and discouragement which sometimes seem so natural. Do this by briefly changing your occupation and busying yourself with thoughts, readings and conversations which make the mind happy and elevate it. Do not pretend to drown melancholy in alcohol for, as a modern author says, drinking does not drown our troubles but only irrigates them.

The central powerhouse which supplies current to our organs is optimism, either instinctive or acquired. Feelings of joy and health stimulate blood circulation and accelerate nutritional processes. If you doubt your forces and think yourself sick, you are already beginning to be sick. Then the central powerhouse has lowered its potential. All lights grow dim. Your organs do not work so well. Sad passions, such as fear, worry, discouragement, agitation, anger, scorn, anxiety, make us realize the truth in the common phrase, "It makes me sick!"

All joy is curative and all discouragement tends to increase our troubles. Gladness is a swimming pool of health where we should bathe each day. Chapter XIV of this book (on happiness) will help you produce this effect.

Get Down To Work

If you suffer from any of these personality maladjustments remember that there is no lesion in your higher faculties, above all in your will. What happens is that you do not know how to use them. These faculties are marvelous forces. When well directed they are capable of transforming any mental pattern and curing any abnormality. But you must know how to avail yourself of their benefits. This is easily attained by re-education. You have the cure in your own hands. A little constancy and method is enough.

Your thoughts are the limit of your activities. No one takes a single step further than his convictions. If you imagine to yourself that you cannot do this or that, you will never do it. *"Possunt quia posse videntur,"* the old Romans used to say. "They can because they think they can." Aside from the times when you need the ministrations or advice of a professional physician, your six best doctors are sun, water, air, exercise, diet and joy. They are always there waiting for you. They cure your ills and do not cost you a cent.

PART TWO

•

Re-Education and Applications

The kind of life many of us are forced to live in the modern world is fatiguing and hinders rest even in sleep. It makes tranquil and deep thought more difficult. It stifles the will and confuses acts of the will with mere impulses. It exalts feelings, lets the sexual instinct run riot, kills all deep satisfaction and true happiness. It deadens or annihilates ideals. The following applications and methods of re-education, personality readjustment and self-completion follow logically from the first part of this book.

VII

How to Rest

Whoever knows how to rest at the right time will double his efficiency and not waste his health.

REST MEANS the suspension of work and energy output, the recuperation of energy and building up of reserve forces. We must learn how to rest: (A) *While awake:* at odd moments, during meal times, while traveling, during the time of recreation, as part of our social and religious life, and even at certain moments during our work itself. We must also learn how to rest. (B) *During the hours of sleep.*

WHILE AWAKE

1. In an acute crisis of "overwork" or nervous fatigue.
2. In normal fatigue.

(1) Nervous Fatigue

We can consider the brain cells as accumulators of energy. They are normally charged when the blood carries oxygen and nutrition to them during the repose of sleep. This would also take place on other occasions when we maintain a mental and emotional disinterestedness while also in a state of muscular relaxation. This is a comparison or theory not yet scientifically proven, but put forward as an hypothesis. These cells would discharge their energy whenever we turn our active attention upon anything.

This discharge of energy is slow and almost imperceptible in the spontaneous and peaceful attention had in conscious sensations or simple concentration. It is something like electricity consumed by a lamp of low wattage. Then the brain cells hardly consume any appreciable amount of our energy.

The discharge of energy will be greater and more noticeable in the case of violent or forced attention (compare burning a high-powered electric light). Another instance would be the case of having one thing at the center of our conscious attention (e.g., something that we hear or read) and, at the same time, some other subconscious center of attention such as a vague scruple, a hidden problem, a stifled fear or disgust, or a need to hurry (compare two candles, one well lit and the other sputtering). The brain cells are expending more energy than normal.

But the discharge of energy will be most rapid when, instead of a single lamp or a lamp and a half, two lights are burning full power at the same time. That is to say, when we have two centers of conscious attention, as a person who wants to pay attention to several matters at the same time![1] Now the brain cells are consuming even their reserve energy.

---

[1] Probably there is no such thing as a simultaneous and fully conscious attention to two or more matters at the same time, but rather a *very rapid shift back and forth* from one idea to another.

If the battery power is greaty expended but not entirely, because we interrupt it in time or because we soon correct the double attention, we do feel mental fatigue, but we recuperate easily. The fatigue will be greater and recuperation more difficult if our reserves become exhausted. This will especially be true if the "accumulator" is only half charged because of an illness or general weakness, or because the forced attention is prolonged a great deal, or because the "double lamp" consumes too much energy.

A student may be already exhausted by successive nights of forced study just before an examination. Or a businessman or professional man may be nervous and irritated to the point of exploding because of worry, anxiety and hurrying. If either of these goes on demanding more and more energy from himself, his cells will have had no time to replenish themselves and will have nothing more to give. They will go on to consume their very substance in order to provide all the energy possible, and he will soon experience true exhaustion or "surmenage" (overwork). This is more difficult to cure as the internal self-consumption has progressed. In extreme cases some tissues can even start to break down. Then the feeling of fatigue, accompanied by a sensation of heaviness or heat in the forehead or around the eyes, and followed by sad and depressing ideas, is unusually intense and difficult to control. Consequently, the first remedy is to take adequate means to get the patient to forget himself and his illness. Specialists obtain this effect organically and violently by injections or electric shocks which produce forgetfulness or artificial sleep. However, in many less serious cases we need not take such extreme measures.

Similar results can be obtained through less violent and more natural means; for example, a few days' travel or a change of dwelling or occupation. Enliven yourself with amusements which will arouse enthusiasm and prevent depressing memories. Avoid remaining inactive or unoccupied. Idleness is no solution. If depressing feelings find the field of consciousness unoccupied they will at once occupy it themselves and begin to torment you. In short, be objective. Act during the day as a receiver of impressions from the external world so that you give no place or time to the interior world of subjective thoughts and feelings. Later on let the work of re-education begin by means of conscious sensations and voluntary concentrations.

In Normal Fatigue

Since this comes from the working of your productive power, make yourself receptive by means of conscious sensations.

Apply the sense of *sight*. Let the object penetrate within you exactly as it is, without subjective modifications. Make no comparisons. Do not reason about causes and effects. Otherwise you will still be producing ideas. Look at things just as children do, naturally, without anxiety, without wanting to embrace all the details. Contemplate, for example, a lamp, a landscape, a flower, a color, the details of some object. Get the overall effect. Absorb yourself in it. With practice this will, day by day, become easier and more successful.

Hear a near or distant noise. Retain consciousness of it for a few seconds. Or even notice the lack of noise. Open up the sense of hearing without forced attention. Repeat these acts five times each hour of the day. With these exercises you can calm irritation and hypersensitivity to sound.

Touch and feel the coldness or hardness of five objects. In each case notice the first impression on the sense.

Walk slowly, deliberately. An excellent relaxing exercise is that used by a student who had a bad case of overwork. He could scarcely pay attention to what he was doing for more than three quarters of an hour. He had to attend three classes a day which were interrupted by five-minute recess periods. These he dedicated to scientific breathing and exercise. He would take five steps while inhaling deeply through the nose, feeling the air in the upper part of the nose near the forehead (not at the nostril openings for this closes them). Then he would exhale smoothly and passively through the mouth while taking eight or ten steps more. Meanwhile he kept his attention on hearing the air as it passed through his nose, and feeling his steps. By thus keeping himself *merely receptive* for the space of five minutes he would rest from the preceding class. The pure air and increased circulation of his blood freed his system of many toxins.

Rest by the right use of leisure time.[2] As we have said before, idleness is no solution. (Doubtless you have also heard it called "the devil's workshop.") In both normal and excessive fatigue "just doing nothing" brings no real rest. A change of occupation is more restful than merely stopping work. The right

---

[2] The translator has thought the "change of occupation" idea, several times indicated by the author, so worth emphasizing in a place of its own that he has taken the liberty of inserting this and the following paragraph. To the reader is recommended the brilliant essay of Josef Pieper, *Leisure, the Basis of Culture*, New York: Pantheon, 1952.

use of leisure time will do much for your health, happiness, efficiency, concentration and longevity. You will become more interested and more interesting.

Manual workers should make a hobby of one of the fine arts, one of the sciences, social work, a parish activity, or investigate the world of books or new fields of knowledge. Those, on the other hand, whose work is mostly intellectual should, for part of their leisure time, take up some outdoor occupation or hobby which involves more or less vigorous physical exercise. If this is difficult they should at least make a hobby of some manual skill (one of the handicrafts or applied arts). Those who must work with their heads will thus gain greater benefit than by merely turning to some different field of intellectual endeavor. They should also do something with their hands.

You can rest from excessive work by engulfing yourself in studies or occupations or hobbies which amuse and interest you. In these you will easily obtain tranquil and perfect concentration. Another way is deliberately to experience some affection; for example, love of parents, brothers or sisters. This is why a mother who loves her child really rests while working for him. Acts of reverence, confidence, love of God in prayer also produce these good effects. Try to have a loving feeling of His Divine Presence everywhere, especially in yourself and your neighbors, through sanctifying grace.

Bodily Relaxation

The foregoing exercises will help to avoid mental tension. But joined with this tension or caused by it, there is another, a muscular and nervous tension in hands, feet and diaphragm, and especially in the eyes. If through proper exercises you relax these members suitably, you will experience greater mental rest.

Nervous and Muscular Rest.—Tension, worry and overexertion easily have repercussions throughout the whole nervous system, and more especially in the eyes, by putting into a state of abnormal contraction the nerves and muscles which are scarcely ever wholly relaxed even in sleep. If you relax your mind, you will more easily relax those muscles. Likewise, if you let muscles and nerves go loose and limp, your mind will be relaxed and relieved. Since the soul is intimately united to the body, it is logical that any modification in one will modify and influence the other.

You should then relax every muscle. Let them go limp. Begin with the forehead. This will lose its wrinkles or nervous contractions if you loosen up the eyes, letting the eyelids softly fall over them. Continue with the mouth, letting the corners curve up, not down. Loosen up the tongue (make a sagging face like a stupid person's). Let the hands fall softly and leave the fingers loose and limp. Place your foot on the ground with no extra effort. Loosen the muscles of neck, jaws, chest and abdomen. This is also an ideal exercise for inducing sleep. Gymnastic exercises and massaging can also produce this relaxation.

Rest by Rhythmical Breathing.—This includes three steps: inhaling, exhaling, then resting motionless. The greatest relaxation is had at the third moment.

One day in New York, after having given four lectures, I found myself exhausted by mid-afternoon with two other lectures still to give. I stretched out on a couch, breathed in deliberately, exhaled naturally, and then deliberately rested for some moments until the body demanded another intake of air. During these brief moments of rest, I deliberately relaxed my eyes, forehead and all my muscles. After a few breaths, I fell asleep. Ten minutes later I woke up completely refreshed and with the same mental lucidity as if I had spent a night in bed.

Resting the Vision.—The eyeball's many nerves and accommodation muscles grow tense through worry, anxiety or mental tension. If you do not relax them before going to bed, they will not loosen up at all during sleep, especially if the previous tension has been profound or prolonged. When this goes on for weeks and months, they finally lose their elasticity. They will then be unable to accommodate the eye as they should. Farsightedness, nearsightedness and bad focusing will result. In order to relax them we here propose several exercises recommended by experience and by the eye-specialist, Dr. Bates.

1. Palming. Sit down comfortably and relax your whole body. Let your eyelids fall softly and close the eyes without pressure. Think of the eyeball as soft, limp and free of tension. Think that a smile is spreading evenly throughout the closed eyes. Imagine there is no light at all in them, that everything is soft and black. Cover them with the palms of your hands. Cup your hands a little so as not to press on the eyeball. Put your knees rather close

together and lean your elbows on them. Relax the
breathing muscles.

The important thing is for the eyes to be closed,
well covered and as relaxed as possible. The blacker
the color seen, the better relaxation and rest. Your
mind should also rest at the same time. Either let
it wander on pleasant subjects or imagine that the
darkness is growing blacker and blacker. Ten or
twenty minutes of this, two or three times a day
will produce great bodily and mental rest and will
sometimes alleviate and even cure farsightedness.

If you are agitated or tired at bedtime, you should
sacrifice a part of your sleep in order to relax your
eyes. As a result you will sleep much better.

2. *Blinking.* Do this for about ten seconds. This
rest nature claims spontaneously. Fixed, staring eyes
are positively unnatural. This is a harmful habit and
causes fatigue and tension.

3. *Cold-water baths.* This relaxing effect can also
be obtained by splashing a few handfuls of water
on your closed eyes.

After these exercises open your eyes and take a
look around. Let the vision of an object or book
come to you of itself and rest within your eye. Do
not, as it were, reach out after it. Effort to see
hinders our seeing well.

The normal eye does not attempt to see a large
amount all at the same time. Practice looking for
example, not at a whole line but at a word or phrase.
The eyes' movements are so rapid that we get the
impression that they cover a great space at once.
But when you try to see everything at once, your
eyes are in a state of tension. Relax and let them

go limp if you wish to see without fatigue. In reading you should use your eyes as you do in writing. You do not then put on the pressure but watch each word as you write it. So, in reading and seeing, you should take in every detail in its own time and not be in hurry to see the whole thing at once.

After all illnesses the eyes, too, are convalescent. In a general weakness or fatigue these, too, are weak. At such times you should not make them work as if they were in perfect condition. Reading is one of the most difficult tasks for the eyes. The sick should read only a little bit or for short spaces of time. They should frequently close their eyes for a few minutes' rest. They should never make an effort to read. If you are suffering from mental or nervous fatigue, you should never read without first resting for fifteen minutes of sleep or for twenty minutes with your eyes closed. Then read with your eyes relaxed. Read for only a short time at a stretch and stop for rest when you come to periods or paragraph endings.

REST WHILE ASLEEP

Sleep, as we said above, includes both a suspension of work, which is the discharge of energy, and the recuperation of energy and reserve strength. This is most perfectly accomplished by perfect sleep without dreams or nightmares. The reasons for this follow:

1) In sleep the work of the brain is suspended (thoughts, images, feelings) and especially its function of relating to one another the different experiences of life. Only automatic movements take place and changes of bodily position. If any muscle is not

sufficiently relaxed, we feel pain or stiffness in it when we waken. During sleep spontaneous sensations and subconscious life diminish and even cease in proportion to the depth of the sleep and the extent of our muscular relaxation.

2) In sleep the functions of our vegetative life diminish without being suspended. Respiration is slower, deeper and more rhythmical. Less blood circulates to the brain. Throughout the whole organism the discharge of energy is minimal.

3) On the other hand, there is an increase in the recuperating activity of the nerve cells and blood (more red blood cells are produced). The body's defenses against microbes are more efficient and impurities are eliminated from the bloodstream by the activity of liver and kidneys.

Distinction between Rest and Sleep.—Without rest we cannot live; without sleep we can. In other words, without suspending the discharge of energy and without recuperating energy, we cannot for long maintain our activity or even our life. But even without a complete loss of consciousness, if we do stay in bed with absolute disinterestedness and mental peace and perfect muscular relaxation, we shall achieve an 80, 90 or greater percentage of rest during the night. If we call perfect sleep 100 per cent rest, we would term a restless sleep or one with nightmares no more than a 70 or 60 or less percentage of recuperation.

Consequently, we need not worry so much about insomnia. Rather we should learn how to rest well. In other words, we should not go to bed to sleep, but to rest. We should pay more attention to the quality of sleep than to its quantity. Five hours of perfect rest would often be enough to make up for daily fatigue. Even if we do not sleep at all, but stay in bed and deliberately relax all our muscles (which often maintain a residual tension even in sleep), we shall learn how to obtain a greater degree of rest in the future. In such a state of perfect relaxation we can achieve a high degree of mental and emotional stasis and recuperate almost as much energy as if we had spent the night in sleep. And on the following day we shall be able to work normally.

The head of a large college began to suffer from insomnia because of illness. At first he was a bit worried. But then he said to himself, "If I can't sleep, at least I am going to rest in bed." He went about this with perfect bodily relaxation and peace of mind. Weeks and months passed without this forcing him to give up his job. He admitted to me that for six months he could not remember having slept for a minute with total lack of consciousness. When he finally lost his fears of insomnia and no longer worried about the absence of sleep, gradually sleep began to return to him.

Sleep with dreams, and especially with nightmares, is no longer perfect repose. For the brain is then unconsciously working. This work can even cause fatigue.

Duration of sleep.—This should vary according to the age and constitution of each individual. As a general norm we can say that when the organism is in a period of development more than seven hours seems needful. Babies and little children need more than ten. Adolescents should have from eight to ten, and young people from seven to eight. For adults seven hours are recommended, although, according to noted authors and the experience of many, only five hours would be sufficient. Total satiation with sleep makes some nervous people more apt to lose control because they find it more difficult to go to sleep next time.

Dreams

The cause of dreams can be bodily (a position of the body which oppresses the heart, bad digestion, general weakness) or mental. The latter may be lack of control over the day's acts and ideas, especially those which immediately precede sleep, or working with concomitant anxiety or parasite ideas, or strong impressions, worries, emotional conflicts, unresolved problems, remorse of conscience, or strong impressions from movies, novels or horror stories.

External circumstances are an occasion, rather than the cause, of insomnia. We know this because in identical circumstances some people will sleep while others do not. Examples of such external circumstances are mosquitoes, loud noises, someone else's snoring, too much light, heat or cold, a strange bed, and so forth. Certain internal circumstances may also prevent sleep, such as sickness, hardening of the arteries, advanced rheumatism, toothache, stomach ache, bad circulation, or too much alcohol, tobacco, or coffee.

Causes of Insomnia

Physiological Cause.—Observe someone asleep in a chair, his eyes closed, his head drooping, his arms and fingers relaxed. This observation tells us that we must relax the muscles in order to sleep. If these remain tense, sleep will be difficult. Muscular tension, then, is the immediate physiological cause of insomnia. But muscular tension is a result of nervous excitement deriving from ideas and feelings. The physiological mechanism responsible for sleep has not been isolated. Many have believed that sleep is due to a separation of the dendrites (nerve endings) or an interruption of nerve currents which takes place when conscious activity ceases. Others explain it in terms of a harmony between the activity of the sympathetic and parasympathetic nervous systems.[3] When the activity of the first which predominates in the state of wakefulness is checked or diminished by mental tranquility and relaxation, it comes into equilibrium with the activity of the second until sleep is finally produced. The part played by the hypothalamus in this procedure is generally admitted today.

Mental Cause.—In any theory, however, what produces this excitation or overactivity of the sympathetic nervous system is excessive work on the part of your productive power. Today it may be an uncontrolled fixed idea or an associated train of ideas corresponding to what you see and hear dur-

---

[3] The *sympathetic* nervous system is made up of two cords, one on either side of the spinal column, and connected by nerve fibers with the external blood vessels, glands, smooth muscles, etc. One of its functions is to speed up the heart.

The *parasympathetic* nervous system is made up of two groups of nerves arising in the cranial and sacral regions respectively. These have among their functions the constricting of the pupils, dilating of blood vessels, slowing of the heart and increasing the action of the glands and disgestive and reproductive organs.

ing the day. Tomorrow it may be some emotional conflict or a simple fear of the insomnia experienced before. Another time it might be an annoyingly unpleasant noise, such as another person's snoring or a neighbor's radio.

It is a big mistake to say, "Go to sleep quickly for there isn't much time." Given to a person (or to oneself) on the way to bed, this order is more likely to produce the opposite effect. Because going to sleep is an unconscious process, we make it more difficult by trying to bring the will into it. The less you think about it, the better. Sleep is like your shadow; if you go after it, it flees from you.

Remedies for Insomnia

Drugs and Sleeping Pills.—These are not cures, but palliatives. They merely help us to get out of a difficulty. They should be used only in exceptional cases, for a brief time, and under medical direction. They do not cure, but leave us weaker in the struggle against insomnia. The true remedy is a double one: the elimination of mental and nervous excitement, and muscular relaxation.

MENTAL REST

1. When going to bed you should put up the following imaginary sign to oppose your worries, excitements or business of the day: "Closed temporarily for repairs." In other words, you have to cut every mental or emotional connection with the day's events. Let every idea slip away. Let no thought bring you fear or desire. When you have pressing problems, serious worries, or emotional conflicts, we must find their solution beforehand. Bedtime is not the time to look for the answers. At most you should then decide to wait till the next day to solve or accept them.

2. *Eliminate a fixed idea or train of ideas.*—Once in bed, or just beforehand, repel this fixed idea or interrupt the train of ideas by filling your consciousness with sensations (receptive mental activity). If there is an emotional conflict, discover where it is and dissolve it in the same way.

3. *Eliminate the subconscious fear of not sleeping.* After a night or several nights of insomnia you go to bed with a fear and anxiety about not sleeping. This may also be present even when you seem to have an interior resignation. Your breathing is not entirely free or deep. Your muscular relaxation is not complete. This anxiety or fear is what is enslaving you. Even though it seems strange, the best remedy is to ask you *to will not to sleep* for a fixed length of time (one or two hours). If your decision or promise is sincere, you will notice at once that the hidden anxiety is gone. The breathing which was rather short before is now more natural and deeper. Once the fear of not sleeping is gone (now that you yourself *want* not to sleep), your productive power stops working on that idea. The activity of your sympathetic nervous system diminishes, and you consequently feel the sensation of sleep coming on. But, notice, you should be faithful to your pledge and resist sleep during the time determined. Otherwise the penalty will be to make this remedy useless when another occasion arises. If the fear reappears when you try to go to sleep again, repeat the same procedure even if you have to sacrifice sev-

eral hours, or a whole night or several nights. It is certain that you will win out in the end.

Do not give too much importance to sleep by thinking that a certain number of hours is indispensable. Sometimes a simple mental sleep is sufficient (making yourself merely receptive, with muscular relaxation and rhythmic breathing). Edison, the inventor, used to work all night, but would take several ten-minute cat-naps during the day.

BODILY REST

Relax the muscles: The organic part of the remedy is to relax all the muscles, beginning with the eyes.

1. The eyes should only be closed, without any pressure. This is easy when we go to bed in normal fatigue, but becomes difficult when sleep does not come as soon as usual. Similarly when we awaken in the middle of the night or at early dawn and wish to go back to sleep. Then the danger is that we shall try to force the eyes shut. Instead, keep them open but relaxed until they close of themselves.

2. The eyes themselves should be relaxed and not fixed or staring behind the eyelids. Pretend that you are looking up and back or that you are letting them turn up and back. This will help you to relax the muscles which control the eyeballs.

3. To help the other facial muscles to relax, make a kind of a "stupid face." Let the lower jaw droop, the cheeks and upper lip rise a bit, and the tongue lie upon the lower jaw (and not compressed against the upper part of the mouth). Some people sleep with their jaws clenched. When they go to bed, they should yawn deliberately a few times, opening the mouth wide. Yawning is a good sleep-producer because of the perfect breathing and relaxation it induces.

4. Relax the other muscles, too: parts of the neck, arms, hands, legs, feet and toes. Let them lie as if they were dead, without any movement, with only the pull of gravity affecting them.

5. Imitate the slow, deep and rhythmical breathing of a sleeper, keeping these three steps: inhaling, exhaling, then resting before you inhale again until the organism needs another breath. At such moments of rest you will notice that you can relax your eyes, forehead, etc., much more easily. Many people who tried this method after hearing one of my lectures told me later that they fell asleep after the tenth breath, even after suffering from insomnia for years.

6. If there has been great nervous excitement before going to bed, for instance after a public appearance, a great fright, a quarrel, or after losing one's temper, you must calm down and get the excitement under control *before* going to bed. Twenty minutes are enough for this if you prevent your memory from getting you excited all over again. For about twenty minutes practice conscious acts or conscious sensations or concentrate your attention on something easy and pleasant. Then you will be able to calm down after the greatest excitement.

7. *Eliminate the annoyance of noise.* When you find you are annoyed by a noise (another's snoring, traffic noises, the ticking of a clock, a neighbor's radio), notice that the racket is not the cause but only a condition of insomnia. For we sleep on a train with

a great deal more noise going on. The immediate
and true cause is the ideas which the noise awakens in us and which we do not control (indignation,
impatience, anxiety to sleep). The remedy lies in
willing to hear the noise. Make yourself a voluntary
receiver of it, without subjectively modifying it with
other ideas. The sense of hearing has sound as its
proper object. It should then be able to find its
satisfaction in it.

During a pilgrimage I was sharing my room with
another. Hardly had he gone to bed than he began
to snore loudly enough to waken the dead. At first
I started to be impatient. Then I applied the
remedy. I willed to listen to the snoring and hear it
clearly, tranquilly observed it and a little later fell
asleep. Waking up once during the night (the noise
was terrific), I used the same method again and
returned to sleep.

OTHER BODILY AIDS

1. Early rising and physical exercises during the day.

2. A frugal evening meal: milk, eggs, vegetables
rich in vitamins, phosphorus, and calcium; few fats
or fried foods.

3. Digestion finished before bedtime.

4. After supper avoid prolonged or taxing mental
work.

5. A moderate walk in the evening or simple gymnastics just before going to bed.

6. If there is tension in the eyes, practice "palming"
them.

7. Provoke yawning by opening the mouth wide and
stretching the throat.

8. Sometimes it is helpful to bathe one's face or take a shower followed by a brisk toweling. This calms the nerves and brings more blood to the skin.

9. No serious reading in bed.

Résumé on Sleep

Before going to bed: avoid excitement or strong emotions. If they happen, calm down before you go to bed.

Going to bed: 1) mental and emotional stasis; 2) relax the muscles beginning with eyes, forehead, jaw, etc.; 3) breathe rhythmically, slowly and deeply, imitating a sleeper; 4) pay attention calmly to your breathing and relaxation.

In bed: 1) know how to use mental rest as well as sleep; 2) do not make sleep itself too important.

Avoid Voice Fatigue

Many orators, teachers, actors, singers and other professional public speakers (and this can happen even as a result of prolonged private conversation) talk for a long time in a loud voice and then feel fatigue, a sensation of oppression in the chest, throat irritation or hoarseness, and sometimes back-pains and other discomforts. They force their voice unnaturally and become exhausted after a half hour of speaking in public. Many have abandoned their profession or crippled their performance for this very reason. If they only knew the organic and mental causes of this defect, they could correct it.

The immediate cause is organic, i.e., defective breathing due to muscular tension. And the root of this tension is connected with uncontrolled emotions. A good voice is based upon a column of air which is kept steady by the abdominal and back muscles and goes out of the nose and mouth without impediment. The voice will not be robust and natural unless the column of air has enough pressure, can be kept steady for the length of a paragraph, and there is no physical impediment to its projection.

Organic Cause.—The organic cause is defective because of muscular tension; above all we need an abundant supply of air.

1. There will not be *an abundant supply of air* if there is tension in nose and throat. If the nostrils are pinched together because of an emotional condition, obviously the intake of air will not be strong enough. In such instances we try to compensate by forcing the throat and vocal chords, and this produces fatigue. First of all, then, we must try to open up the nasal passages, especially up above near the eyes. A nose "like a rabbit's" should be the motto, both for inhaling and exhaling.

2. A solid base for the column of air. The base is not there unless the muscles of the lower abdomen and back are well expanded. To expand them, practice breathing from the diaphragm. To check that this is being done correctly place your hands flat against your sides and the fingers will tend to separate when you inhale. Also try to widen the lower curvature of the back. These muscles also come into play by a reflex action whenever we hold the cheek muscles high and keep the nasal passages and palate well open.

3. A steady column of air. The whole air supply should not be gone when we pronounce a single word or phrase. And so we should keep the ribs and lower abdomen dilated and relax them a little bit at a time. Above all we must keep the nasal passages open.

4. The air should be projected without any nasal impediments. It should vibrate a little while we are speaking. The words should come out as if they were blown out or as if we were throwing them out in front of our eyes. The muscles around the cheek-bones must not be squeezed down, nor the upper lip be tense, and the mouth should be opened wide.

5. We should relax other tensions in the chest, shoulders and shoulder blades; otherwise we lessen the chest capacity. Hold the shoulders back and low. The shoulder blades should tend to come together. The rear part of the chest should be lightly elevated rather than thrown out in front, and the lower abdomen somewhat tense. Check that your posture is correct by standing up against a wall with heels back against the wall, and shoulders and head against the wall, naturally and without excessive tension. In many persons who lead a sedentary life, the muscles of waist and back become tense and cramp their breathing. They should practice exercises or massage which relax the waist and back.

Mental or emotional cause.—Emotional states such as terror, worry, hurry, discouragement, anger and so forth tend to shorten our breath. They prevent it from beginning in the lower abdomen as it should. They tighten up the lower curvature of the back and make that difficult to expand. The shoulders rise and bend forward. The lungs, the lower lip, and the corners of the mouth all droop. As a result air does not enter or leave with ease. Hence, the voice's resonance and volume are lost; for these depend upon all the breathing muscles being flexible. You may recall the awkward tone of voice of timid people. The positive emotions, on the other hand, of love, joy, security, and optimism dilate the chest and lungs, make us breathe better and help us to produce vocal tones more freely and purely.

Practical Exercises for Relaxing the Voice

First adopt the correct posture as indicated above: body erect, lower abdomen not protruding, lower back straight, upper chest expanded, shoulders held back and low, shoulder blades close together, facial muscles relaxed, upper lip and cheek muscles raised, nose and throat opened.

1. Breathe deliberately through the nose and let the air come out naturally through the nose (10 times or so).

2. Breathe the same way, but, as the air comes out through the nose, hum lightly until you feel the nasal passages vibrate (10 times or so). Repeat this exercise several times a day for several days until it becomes a habit.

3. Do the same thing, but add after the hum an "O" and then an "A," letting the "O" and the "A" resonate in the head and forehead.

4. Hum again, adding E, I, U.

5. Hum-ta, te, ti, to, tu. Hum-ba, be, bi, bo, bu, etc.

6. First produce the humming vibration, then read aloud a few words or phrases or an entire paragraph, preserving the same "hum" attitude in the face.

Especially when speaking in public you should open your mouth wide, put a great deal of movement in your lips, breathe through mouth and nose both, and pronounce all syllables decisively and distinctly. This will be more easily done, through spontaneous reflexes, when you have trained your whole body to hold a correct posture habitually.

OUTLINE DIAGRAM

⊷⊶

How to Rest

R E S T	1. Stopping the discharge of energy	Normal discharge with one idea Abnormal discharge with two ideas
	2. Recuperating energy by	Tranquil sleep 100% rest Disturbed sleep 60–70% rest Relaxation (Disinterestedness) 90% rest
W H I L E **A W A K E**	Abnormal Fatigue or Exhaustion	Forgetfulness: drugs, change of dwelling or occupation. Re-education { Not by idleness, nor a stress on subjective life, But by pleasant conscious activity.
	In Normal Fatigue	Conscious sensations and conscious activity Pleasant concentrations Exercise and breathing Relaxing the muscles and eyes Moderate affection
	What to look for	Not sleep, but rest Not quantity, but quality
I N **S L E E P**	Duration	Depending on the climate, one's temperament, or job: —a mature organism: five to seven hours; —a developing organism (children, adolescents): 8 to 12 hours.
	Causes of Dreams	Sleeping positions, weakness, illness; Problems, emotions, excitement.
	Sleeping Position	Head to one side, mouth shut, no nervous tossing; Good support from mattress, full relaxation.
	Occasion: Bodily Causes	Noises, etc. Tension, excitement, activity of the hypothalamus.
I N S O M N I A	Mental Causes	Emotions, problems, strong feelings, boiling ideas, anxiety to sleep, fear of insomnia.
	Remedies	Mental and emotional disinterestedness Relaxation of eyes, face, limbs.
VOICE FATIGUE		Surface cause: defective breathing and muscular tension. Deeper cause: emotional crises. Remedies and practical exercises.

VIII

Use of the Will

IRRATIONAL ANIMALS come perfect from the hand of the Creator. By merely following their instincts they develop and reach their goal. They have no need of education. But man is born incomplete. If he follows his animal instinct alone, he weakens himself, sickens and dies. For this purpose God gives him reason, first that of his parents and teachers, then afterwards his own. God says to him, "Complete yourself." Man's duty then will always be to perfect himself, educate, complete and gain the mastery of himself.

The need for education is founded in the struggle between the lower level of mental activity and the higher. The lower level has an appetite only for sense goods, even to the prejudice of higher goods. The higher level of mental activity is capable of knowing and attaining higher goods which are beyond normal sensible experience, are true and eternal. These are goods of the soul, social goods and divine goods.

THE WILL AND MENTAL ACTIVITY

As a compass (or sort of gun-sight) for direction in your own education or that of another, keep in mind these two principles: (1) intense mental acts remain behind within us, and (2) there is a triple scale of values in normal mental activity.

The Persistence of Mental Acts

Every intense mental act contributes to formation or deformation of personality or character. It remains associated with acts which preceded it. Even though unconscious or forgotten, it continues to influence your personality by making related acts more easy and contrary ones more difficult. For the same reason virtues practiced in childhood or at any other time will form within your personality a definite framework of mind. By this you are more apt to act well and efficiently than if this practice had never existed. Likewise a transgression or concession to exaggerated instincts, even if made only once and during youthful folly and even with a resolve to return straightway to the right road, will leave forever within your mental framework a greater inclination to evil and less ease in doing good. A single fault or passing sin is then of no little importance. This is true even though it later incurs no penalty. Nor is any act of virtue unimportant even if it is hidden or unrewarded.

Triple Scale of Values in Normal Mental Activity

The Whole Should Prevail over the Part.—Just as we amputate a gangrenous limb in order to save the whole body, so partial tendencies must be subordinated to the activity of the whole. The special difficulty here arises from the following.

(1) You are dependent on matter as regards food, rest and bodily appetites. These must be brought

into harmony with the spirituality of the soul. Hence, we must restrain gluttony (our tendency to eat or drink too much) in order to care for the health of body and vigor of soul by means of temperance and even fasting. Hence, too, we must overcome sloth, our exaggerated tendency to get too much rest, or toward pleasant pastimes or entertainment. This we do by diligent and disciplined activity. Hence, in addition, we must control the sexual instinct by submitting it through chastity to reason and God's law. We must sacrifice the pleasure of a moment and only one part of the body for the total good of the same. At stake here are mental lucidity, an elevated affective life, and especially the temporal and eternal good of one's soul (see the following chapters).

(2) Our subjection to automatism (tics, fears, spontaneous exaggerated disgusts), slavery to vice or to long-standing habits, exaggerated respect for what others do or "what they will say," all these tend to take the place of our higher liberty and what reason or God have shown us to be obligatory or truly satisfying. ("Judge for yourselves," said the Apostles to the chiefs of the synagogue, "whether it be reasonable for us to obey you or God.") Every form of dictatorship or totalitarianism, and especially Communism, tends to annihilate such true liberty.

(3) The course of our thinking is fantastic when under the influence of emotion. But this must be harmonized with objective truth. Hence, we must regain control of an uncontrolled imagination or a tendency to daydream, of exaggerated fears or sadness, or the hatreds and antipathies which deform reality for us. Even schisms and heresies have had

their origin more in emotion than in objective reasoning.

What Is Objective and Real Should Prevail over What Is Subjective.—In the beginning a child lives enclosed in his own personality. He does not want to do service or give himself. He is an egoist, merely subjective. Normal development or education will bring him to the recognition and realization of objective and social values. He will then make them his norm of action. From his social isolation he will lean toward whoever offers him support. He will want to change himself into a useful and working member of the community. Only a morbid mental pattern will make a man an egoist.

Development Should be Continuous.—Your whole being tends to develop progressively, become the master of itself, realize its ideal gradually. The memory, understanding, and even the muscles tend to atrophy if they are not used. A professional man who neglects to perfect his knowledge becomes ineffective and incompetent. On the road of virtue, too, not to go forward is to turn back. Whole civilizations have become drunk with the thought of progress achieved; then at once they began to crumble. Stagnation, softness and vice conquered the Roman Empire more than the barbarians from the north.

You may draw important ascetical conclusions from these principles. (1) If you give up self-conquest and mortification as a means of rising from vice or sin, there will be a regression in your development or progress. (2) The "liberation of your personality toward objective values" (that is, society or God) is in psychology what in asceticism is called self-conquest, humility or charity. The false asceticisms—stoicism, buddhism, spiritism, laicism—all insist upon partial dispositions. They point you toward a closed personality rather than toward an open one as in Christianity. They can as a result turn you aside to morbid and perverse forms of asceticism. But objective and total asceticism is in harmony with normal mental life.

By education you orientate and strengthen your mind in order that it may always tend toward its own higher goods easily, freely and efficiently. To this end you must educate your will.

EDUCATION OF THE WILL BY MOTIVES[1]

Your will is a rational faculty, naturally inclined to the good. Before acting, your understanding must precede it like a torchbearer and show it a good, a motive, a value. Then it will move into action. You should, then, propose goods or values to yourself or those whom you are to educate. These values must not only be objectively such but must be comprehended by the subject (that is, by you) as worthwhile at the present moment. In short, they must be objective, subjective and actual.

Objective Values.—These are real values, good in themselves; for example, what is useful, honorable, pleasant, necessary. These may be sensory goods perceived by the senses, or spiritual goods grasped by the understanding. They may be goods for time

---

[1] See J. Lindworsky, S.J., *Training of the Will*, Bruce, Milwaukee, 1938; and by the same author, *The Psychology of Asceticism*, Newman, Westminster, Md., 1950.

or eternity, partial or total goods, natural or supernatural.

Subjective Values.—These you perceive to be such. They are accommodated to your capacity. In children, because of their undeveloped understanding, these will be largely sensible goods or those with a sensible element. In adolescents and adults they should also be spiritual and supernatural rather than merely material goods. But they should, as far as possible, be reinforced by the imagination and feelings.

The father of a family once told me, "For a long time I could not succeed in getting my three-year-old son to stop slamming the door. He did not understand the motive (that the noise might bother other people). But one day I gave him another reason which he did understand, 'The door is going to break.' From then on he would neither slam it himself nor let anyone else do so. And he repeated to others the motives as he understood it."

Actual Values.—These are the ones found actually present in your mind at the moment of decision and execution. To keep them present, it will help to write down your good resolutions and their motives. Then read them over again from time to time. For lack of this continued motivation there are very frequent failures in school and home. Children who went to Mass for years, even daily Mass, sometimes do not go at all later on when they are older. The reason is that they went before not because of any motive of their own, but because of their educators. They did not themselves make an act of the will to go to Mass.

In short, the motives were not present when the time came for action.

In all languages there are two words which are magnificent, ennobling and effective: "Yes" and "No." Know how to say "Yes" when you are going forward with great strides, and also when you are moving on an uphill road, very slowly yet ever onward. Know how to say "No" without concessions, discussion or wavering. Herein lies growth and strength.

Active Education for Those with Loss of Will Power.—If you do not perform true will-acts, you will scarcely have any idea of them. What you need above all is an internal experience and intimate feeling of these acts. You must then exercise yourself in external acts which require little effort but are mentally perfect. You must make them concrete, feel their possibility, and produce the mental energy needed for decision.

Active Education for All.—You will find it very useful (1) to distinguish true acts of the will from what are not (mere desire, impulse, velleity or vague intention). (2) Make them concrete so as not to be content with a mere desire or plan. (3) Pass gradually from the easy to the difficult so as to feel their possibility, avoid failures (or false acts of the will) and discouragement.

You can also dramatize your will process by considering it as a battle and distinguishing these four stages in it.

(1) *Presentation of the contestants:* what are the

acts I can will or reject? That is, stay in bed when I am called or jump out of it?

(2) *Struggle between the contestants:* discussion of motives for and against. What good or harm does staying there bring me, and what advantages are there in jumping out?

(3) *You can give the victory to whichever one you choose:* feel the possibility of this.

(4) *Victory of one over the other:* leave it as master of the field of consciousness. Imagine with concrete details how you will jump out. Banish the very thought of a possibility of staying in bed (making it impossible for yourself by decision).

The education of the will should not be just a "lighthouse education" which tries only to avoid shipwrecks on the reefs and shoals of opportunity for evil. Nor should it be a merely negative one which is content to correct defects. Far better will be a positive type of education which will always propose some progress to be attained, perfections to be acquired, virtues to be practiced. This provides an increase of joy, enthusiasm and sense of value. *Education lies not so much in making people put what is good into practice as in teaching them to will it and practice it under their own power.*

I had a student who was really basically good but whose will was very weak and vacillating. He was always being punished. I asked him why he made no effort to correct himself. "I want to, Father, but I can't." I examined his act of will. He did not make it concrete or feel the possibility of it. To help him keep silence at the proper times, I proposed that he bite his tongue (lightly of course) on the way from recreation to study, from study to the classroom

or lecture hall. "Can you do that?" "Yes, Father."
By making the thing concrete and feeling its possibility he did make definite will acts, one day to
please me, another to honor the Blessed Virgin, or to
please Our Lord. At night I would ask him, "How
many times did you fail?" "Eight." "Then kiss the
Crucifix eight times and promise not to fail tomorrow." The result was a rapid improvement which
was joyful and complete.

THE IGNATIAN METHOD

The noted Dr. Vittoz had a great admiration for
St. Ignatius Loyola. He believed that Loyola was
three centuries ahead of his time in the fine introspection and effective pedagogy revealed in his
Exercises and *Examens*. The purpose of St. Ignatius
is to make a man perfect. He proceeds according
to the most sublime laws of our higher mental
activity without allowing the lower levels of activity
or disordered feelings to disturb this process. This
is indicated in the very first paragraph of his little
book.[2] To this end he uses the will's legislative
power in the *Exercises* to choose and determine a
concrete way of life. In the *Examens* he uses the
will's executive power to bring this down into
practice.

---

[2] ". . . just as walking and running are bodily exercises, so also
any method of preparing and disposing the soul to remove from
itself all disordered affections (feelings and impulses) and then to
seek and find the divine will in arranging one's life with a view to
the soul's salvation, these are called spiritual exercises."—". . .
*sicut ambulare . . . et currere sunt exercitia corporalia, ita etiam
quilibet methodus praeparandi et disponendi animam ad tollendas
a se omnes affectiones inordinatas, et . . . ad quaerendam, et
inveniendam voluntatem divinam, in vitae suae dispositione, ad
salutem animae, vocantur exercitia spiritualia.*"—*Exercitia Spiritualia,
op. cit.*, pp. 10–12.

The *Exercises* propose motives which are strongest and noblest in themselves and which are reinforced by the feeling of love for Jesus Christ. These motives are to be subjectively felt and adopted by the exercitant. When his higher mental activity has been so directed that passions do not deroute it, then come meditations preparatory to the "Election" (or choice of a way of life). And then come decisions about concrete details of the future way of life.

The executive power of the will has a very efficient instrument in the "particular examen." This is truly a control and stimulus to the will. The particular examen makes us perform true will-acts by making them concrete, each the subject of some one virtue or vice, and in a determined place and time. It makes us feel their possibility and facility by limiting the expenditure of energy and vigilance to a half day at a time. Finally it makes us renew our decision three times a day, and strengthen it by comparison of one examen with another, with contrition when we fail and with love of Jesus Christ. *It is a spiritual treatment which is most efficacious for curing moral illnesses.*

Dr. Schleich, a Protestant, professor of the Faculty of Medicine at Berlin, asserts even more. "I say with all assurance and conviction that with these norms and exercises in our hands we could even today transform our asylums, prisons and mental institutions, and prevent the commitment of two-thirds of the people who are today within their walls."

And so we see that the will is man's conquest of himself, and the education of the will is the strategy of this conquest.

OUTLINE DIAGRAM

How to Use the Will

{ Education necessary { we are born incomplete / the conflict of our instincts

Remember for orientation {
- intense experiences remain
- triple scale of values { whole over the part / objective over subjective / development continuous

E d u c a t e   t h e   w i l l {

By motives {
- propose goods to be attained (motives)
- *objective* (goods in themselves) { sensible / spiritual / eternal
- *subjective* (perceived as such) { in childhood, first / through the senses, / later in the supernatural
- *actual*—actually present { when making a decision / when carrying it out / in continued motivation

Actively {
- for the abulic { internal experience of will act / practice easy external acts
- for everyone { distinguish will act from mere desire, impulse, e‹ / progress gradually to more difficult acts / dramatize the will process / action under one's own power

Ignation method {
- legislative power of will in the *Exercises* { choice in light of great motives / choice made concrete in "Election"
- executive power of will in the *particular examen* {
  - concrete { Some one virtue or vic‹ / in definite place / at determined time
  - possibility felt { half day at a time / renewals of decisi‹ / thrice daily

IX

The Sexual Instinct

EDUCATION OF THE SEXUAL instinct is especially necessary because the lower level of mental activity is antagonistic to the will, is very strong in this matter and there are very frequent powerful exterior incitements to vice.

Difficulty from an Erroneous Attitude

Many let themselves be mastered by the sexual instinct because they think it irresistible or because they are ignorant of the hidden force of their will, others because of an erroneous persuasion that resistance can cause illness. Very many yield because they expect to find satisfaction in it. They expect to satisfy that thirst for the happiness which all humans seek. However, they seldom reflect upon the transitory and cheap aspect of disordered sex pleasure. It cannot fulfill the noble and unlimited aspirations of the spiritual soul. But they discredit the experience of innumerable people who are physically or mentally sick because of this vice. They count for nothing the testimony of the medical profession, sentences of judges and warnings of moralists. All of these show the brutal excesses of this instinct once the reins have been loosened by the first concessions.

And on a higher level, they have no suspicion of the deep joys, delicate feelings, mental clearness and agility of pure souls. They forget the abjection and sadness, despair and emptiness of vice, the tormenting remorse of conscience and the threatened punishment of God.

All education should begin with ideas. When these are modified, then acts are easily corrected. Then by means of acts the feelings and force of the unconscious are controlled.

IS CHASTITY POSSIBLE AND USEFUL FOR YOUTH?

If chastity were not possible and useful, no one could will it in earnest, not even if it were imposed merely for social convenience. For the instinct is a brutal one and that barricade very weak. Yet nothing is more contrary to science and experience. The great Jewish psychiatrist of Zurich, Dr. Brueler, affirms, *"Whoever recognizes that chastity and continence are possible will hardly have any sexual problems to bother him."* Again, the professors of the Faculty of Medicine in Christiania say, "This faculty of medicine has the honor of making the following declaration: The assertion recently put forth by several persons and repeated in newspapers and public gatherings to the effect that a moral life and perfect continence are bad for the health is something that is completely false according to our experience. *We know of no case of sickness or weakness which we could attribute to perfectly pure and moral conduct."*

A document unanimously approved by New York doctors and specialists reads as follows: "In view of the spread of venereal diseases, the results of an unfortunate heredity and the moral evil inseparable from an impure life, we doctors of New York and its environs subscribe unanimously to the declaration *that chastity, a pure life for both sexes, is conformed to the best conditions for physical, moral and mental health.*" In the Brussels International Conference on Sexual Prophylaxis, 260 members unanimously affirmed the following conclusion: *"It is above all necessary to teach male youth that not only are chastity and continence not harmful, but on the contrary these virtues are to be most highly recommended from a purely medical and hygienic point of view."* As long ago as its session of March 22, 1917, the Paris Academy of Medicine insisted on the necessity of making known to youth "that chastity is not only possible but also beneficial and to be recommended for health's sake."

Thus we could multiply testimonials from the most eminent doctors of the entire world in order to silence the pseudo-intellectuals or would-be wise men who take pleasure in spreading the opposite idea. And from still another standpoint we know that what God *commands* all men in the Sixth Commandment *cannot* be impossible or harmful to health.

Moreover, the sexual glands, in addition to their external, propagative function, benefit the organism with the production of hormones specific for the sex of the individual. These hormones are necessary for the physiological well-being of the organism.

A SPECIAL DIFFICULTY

Acts against purity at a tender age, from 6 to 11 years, even without knowledge of their malice, frequently throw the lower mental activity out of equilibrium by fixing in the unconscious an abnormal inclination toward pleasure. Or early indulgence may transfer the instinct to the wrong method or sex (sexual inversions), depending on its first realizations. And it leaves a strong tendency to look for comfort, ease and pleasure in everything, and to flee from a hard life, inconvenience and pain.

Wrong satisfactions during puberty engrave this emotional pattern even deeper. And it results in an unconscious tendency to reproduce images and memories of pleasure. Persons or circumstances similar to those met in past indulgence at once arouse sexual thoughts or tendencies and impulses to realize them. The environment—movies, beaches, magazines or pornographic advertising—multiply these incentives until it is extremely difficult to resist passion. This is a difficulty, yes, but not one which it is impossible to conquer.

REMEDIES

Preventive Remedies.—Watch over children lest they learn or practice dangerous acts, urged on by bad companions or the example of immoral movies and pictures. But do not see sin where there is none, nor arouse a fear or even the idea of danger or temptation where there is really no moral issue. Else you will be responsible for exaggerated or undue excitability, or an obsessing idea of sex. In the case of adolescents who feel the awakening of instinct and are capable of reflection, teach them in private with dignity and clarity the sublime purpose of Providence in the sexual instinct, the possibility and utility of controlling it, and the grave moral obligation not to go beyond its wise norms. We should calm their nascent curiosity and prevent their satisfying it with corrupt companions. We shall then be able to have them elicit that free-will act without which all will be lost.

Curative Remedies.—First of all, if erroneous ideas are held, these of course must be corrected.

To counteract the unconscious influence of feelings toward pleasure, arouse contrary feelings and tendencies by accustoming your body to work, a hard life, mortification and even pain (dignified by Faith), and by withdrawing it from comfort and pleasure. Healthful, vigorous sports are no little aid to this end.

Avoid persons, objects, reading, conversations and spectacles which involve a less pure association of images and tendencies. To will chastity, yet not avoid these incitements, is like setting out to walk on a slippery hill.

When evil tendencies or thoughts appear resist them at the very first moment, "while they are still weak." Do this by opposing other images (conscious sensations, voluntary concentrations, acts which require attention) and other tendencies (wanting to avoid Hell, win Heaven, please Jesus Christ, save souls).

Whenever one very chaste and virtuous young man met friends and relatives of the other sex, he would be disturbed and attracted by impure thoughts without knowing how to avoid them. It was enough to advise him to practice consciously associating other images with the idea of woman— for instance, the excellence of the mother who bears children for Heaven, the Holy Ghost dwelling within her by grace, the sublimity of the Virgin Mother of God. In a few days he returned to express his gratitude. This new, voluntarily induced association of ideas had done away with the other subconscious and instinctive ones and he felt tranquil and happy.

To attain better resistance avoid lower states of mental activity (alcoholism, romanticism, somnolence, mental vagueness, daydreaming). In these your imagination or subconscious feelings have free rein. And your will and reason are, as it were, asleep. Then the whole man is at the mercy of the first impulse. The first impulse will rise up in a rolling wave, especially if you are also in a too comfortable bodily position. This latter, because of an unconscious association with the sense of touch, awakens the lowest instincts. You will indeed have the power to resist even then, and for this reason will be responsible for your acts. The holy Curé of Ars fled the sensation of comfort as if it were fire. We should raise the level of this heroic struggle and not make it out to be merely a negative one: "You may not do this; you must avoid that." Rather put it positively as a sacrifice generously offered to our God who has been crucified for us, to love Him, please Him, obey and imitate Him. This positive struggle brings joy and enthusiasm. A negative approach brings only depression.

Against motor ideas which impel you to perform an impure act, oppose the feeling that you are able to avoid it and the concrete will act of an opposite movement. For example, command your feet not to go into a certain place or your hands to remain crossed on your breast for a definite length of time. Do this in order to strengthen your character, develop your personality, please Our Lady, merit Heaven. (Do nothing "in order to avoid sin," for such a reference will awaken the ideas and impulses which you are trying to control.) Made concrete in this way, you can feel these acts as possible and you will really want them.

Once you have done all you humanly can in this very difficult matter, you still need recourse to God to obtain supernatural strength by prayer, confession and Communion. This grace will never be denied you when you seek it with entire humility, confidence and perseverance. The experience of many centuries, by all races and men of every intellectual and social position, demonstrates that these supernatural means do conquer the special difficulty of remaining chaste.[1]

---

[1] Cf. the encyclical of Pius XII on Holy Virginity (*Sacra Virginitas*), Mar. 25, 1954; and the encyclical of Pius XI on Christian Marriage (*Casti Connubii*), Dec. 31, 1930.

OUTLINE DIAGRAM

❦

How to Train the Sexual Instinct

Possibility
- Testimony: Dr. Brueler
- Faculty of Medicine of Christiania
- Doctors of New York and environs
- International Conference at Brussels
- Paris Academy of Medicine
- God commands it

Difficulty
- Fixation of inclination toward pleasure because of acts performed
- Association of ideas and tendencies

Remedy

Preventive
- watch over children
- instruct adolescents
- stress acts of the will

Curative
- correct erroneous ideas
- form positive tendencies and contrary habits
- avoid incentives
- resist beginnings with
  - other images
  - other tendencies
- avoid states of lower mental activity
- oppose bad impulses with
  - concrete will acts
  - the conviction of triumph
- prayer, confession, Communion

X

Feelings

FEELING IS A FORCE God gives you for willing and working with greater energy and constancy. But, like steam in a locomotive, it is a chaotic force. If well channeled by reason (with its safety valves and opportune expansion and release), it will be exceedingly useful to you.

GENERAL CONTROL

Do Not Let Feelings Govern You

Make no change under the influence of feelings. To have as a norm of action "because I like to" is the same as to take a trolley car or bus without bothering about where it is going or only because it is more comfortable or is shinier than another. Likewise, to stop working "because it is a bother" or "troublesome" is to renounce success, joy, glory and even your own salvation.

> *To want something only because there is no other way out is the way a slave acts.*
> *To want it because it is no trouble (following likes or impulses) is the way an animal acts.*

> *To want it in spite of the bother (guided by*
> *reason or duty) is the way a rational*
> *human being acts.*
> *To want even the bother of it (with your*
> *eyes on the ideal or on God) is the way*
> *a hero or saint acts.*

The child and the socially unadapted person love or hate, work or stop working only because of their likes and dislikes, because reason has not been developed or has been inhibited.

Govern Your Feelings

Restrain exaggeration of feelings. Do not give too much importance to them, or to what pleases or displeases you, or to what you fear or desire. For experience tells us that feeling heightens colors, exaggerates good or evil, obscures and alters truth.

For example, do the words or behavior of another irritate you? Then your feelings will make you tend to think that he has a deliberate bad intention (whereas he probably acted only out of lightmindedness or without full reflection). They will even persuade you that he has yet worse plans for the future. Does the mailman or telegraph messenger bring you bad news? At least your imagination will immediately run riot and overload the unopened envelope with the blackest shadows. "Somebody is dead," you may think. Or, "Some relative has gone bankrupt." Do you feel a little unwell? Your uncontrolled thought will tell you, "It must be tuberculosis, or heart trouble, or the beginnings of insanity." Is it a case of not making progress in your studies, or in

virtue, or prayer? Do you find yourself sad and discouraged and wish to give up the spiritual life you
adopted? Does it seem to you that you were not
made for this? *In all these cases you have lost
control of your feelings by letting them become
exaggerated.* Convince yourself that the real situation is much better than your emotional reaction
to it.

Control Your Thoughts

Do not give free rein to their deceptive argu-
ments. Avoid their exaggerations and transfers to
other fields. Think about something else and, above
all, *do not change your plans or make important
resolutions under the sway of feeling.* Let a day go
by. Let a night go by, too. "Consult your pillow."
Then, when your feelings are calmed, you will be dis-
posed for work and you will see that "the lion is not
so fierce as he is painted." With regard to mental illness as a dreaded possibility one must discount fear;
believe psychiatrists when they say that those who
become demented were the ones who had no fear
of becoming so.

With his fine sense of psychology St. Ignatius
traces out for us three very wise rules for governing
ourselves when a depressing feeling comes over us.

Firstly, in time of desolation (that is, when you are
discouraged or sad, without light or strength, without peace or consolation, or when temptation blinds
you) make no change, but continue with the plans
you made when you had peace, light and consolation.

Secondly, think of the fact that this state will pass
and that light and joy will return. Encourage the

thoughts and feelings you had before the desolation came.

Thirdly, act against the very desolation. Do the opposite of what you feel yourself inclined to do. Lengthen your prayer, for example, or perform even more mortifications.

In the Palace of Feelings there are brilliant halls where dwell optimism, hope, love, valor and joy. And there are dark cellars, lurking places of discouragement, sadness, fear, worry, anger. The mistress of the Palace, the will, has to pass through all its rooms but can delay wherever she wishes. We should not give too much importance to fears or sadness when they come. We should not habitually and voluntarily stay with them, but pass on to the halls of joy and optimism.

Open the Safety Valve

There are states of feeling in which repression can cause fatigue, suffering and illness. Such are the apparent conflicts between the commands of duty and the demands of honor, love or instinct. Frequently the mere manifestation of these to your mental guide or spiritual director will lighten them, reveal the solution and cure them.

During the First World War psychiatrists were surprised to note the greater number of cases of severe mental illness among English soldiers than among the French. They investigated the causes and found that the former had been brought up in the atmosphere of believing that an Englishman should not feel fear and that it would be a national disgrace to give any sign of it. This mentality imposed on many individuals a violent struggle, repression of

unavoidable feelings, and finally mental disequilibrium. When this mentality was modified, there
were fewer victims.

There are four kinds of difficulties or internal conflicts which we should make known as soon as possible to a prudent director lest they poison our wills
or at least tire our minds unnecessarily.

(1) *Acts* which weigh down our conscience with
moral responsibility.

(2) *Worrisome practical doubts* which we cannot
solve, or obsessing temptations to evil.

(3) *Tormenting indecision* in important matters
(this may be a result of the preceding).

(4) *Oppressing fears or sadness* which we do not
know how to control.

When a tumor is opened, the victim is relieved.
So a release of these emotional conflicts with a
prudent friend or spiritual guide and, above all, the
divine release of them in sacramental confession,
roots out of our soul all that poisonous overload. It
brings us so much peace, joy and encouragement
that non-Catholic doctors of different countries agree
that if confession had not been established in the
Church as a spiritual medicine, they would have had
to prescribe it themselves as a treatment for emotional ailments rising from disordered feelings.

You should also open the safety valve of dignified
affection in the expansions of family love, true
friendship, spiritual confidences, love of your neighbor, love of souls, and love of God. All your mental
energy does not flow into the channel of your
understanding when you try to close off or block up
the channel of feeling. There must be some release
of feeling.

**Close the Escape Valve to Brute Instinct
and Disordered Passions**

A fourth-year medical student once came to see
me after a lecture. He could not sleep, study or fix
his attention. He was wallowing in discouragement,
depression and profound sadness. He had to stop
attending classes. He had been studying intensely,
at the same time had to attend to troublesome family
affairs, and was also worrying about an illness of his
father's. He consulted an atheistic psychiatrist who
recommended certain injections and that he give
vent to his sexual instinct. This latter, according
to the diagnosis, was being repressed and was the
cause of his illness. The young man followed this
foolish advice only to find himself even more confused, sad and worried. Once the true cause of
his sickness was found and all was made right
with God through confession, he began the work of
re-education joyfully. He recovered his ability to
sleep in two days.

Apparently there are not a few atheistic psychiatrists who follow Freud (as they say) and want to
re-establish lost equilibrium by subjecting the angel
to the brute, the soul to the body, the higher mental
activities to the lower, the conscious to the unconscious. Dr. Vittoz and his whole school, together
with all spiritual psychiatrists, are in revolt against
such an aberration.

You should also do away with useless confidences
which are born of emotionalism or impulse. Never
recount to any person you meet, just to console yourself, what you suffer or fear, desire or plan. This
might give you some momentary consolation (that

of yielding to the impulse), but the sad ideas will impress you more in the telling and make you more their slave. If you tell them to your friends, you make them sad; if to your enemies, you make them glad. The ills of another, and much less the details of what you suffer, feel or fear, are not of much interest to anyone even though his charity or courtesy lead you to think so. On the other hand, if you forget yourself in the affairs of other people, you will at the same time get your own feelings under control, learn something useful, and acquire an affable and sympathetic personality.

XI

The Power of Wrath

"Iᶠ ʏᴏᴜ ʜᴀᴠᴇ an enemy," says Dr. Fosdick, "or dislike someone, the greatest evil you can do, not to him but yourself, is to allow hatred to sink into your soul and plough a lasting furrow there."

To control the emotion of anger it will be helpful to know its psycho-physiological trajectory. Here we shall diagram only its controllable or voluntary phase, referring the reader to Chapter IV for the diagram of the first or spontaneous phase. Here we are using *anger* as a concrete illustration of the growth and flowering of emotions and feelings.

A. Spontaneous Phase

Injustice, insults, or annoyances affect the cerebral cortex by means of the senses or imagination. If we perceive these as contrary to our life, honor, health or ideals, we form one of the three following judgments.

"I, They, It"

I: "With my good qualities, merits, and intentions, I do not deserve such treatment."

They: "They are unfair, cruel, ungrateful, or unbearable."

It: "It [the event] is unfair, unjust, intolerable, dangerous."

Especially if it is very prolonged and is felt to be very strong, this concrete judgment stimulates the hypothalamus which is the engine room of the emotions. Thence the autonomic nervous system spontaneously goes into action. This, plus the action of sympathin, puts heart, stomach, lungs, muscles, viscera, etc., in hyperactivity. And we are invaded by feelings of disgust and antipathy.

This is an example of what the classical moral philosophers and moral theologians call *motus primo primi*. In it there is no responsibility nor any sin. We really cannot control it except indirectly, and then only with a great deal of vigilance. We can try to avoid the exciting factor, or at least the memory of it, and to shorten its duration. We do find that we are able to avoid making the concrete judgment, "I, They, It," or at least to modify it once it is present in us. This we can do either by deliberately interposing a distraction or, better, by deliberately forming in ourselves a different attitude by means of an adequate education or re-education. If we do this, the disturbance will pass rather quickly without leaving behind a lasting or profound effect.

B. Voluntary Phase

I. Destructive Development.

These disturbances in the organs themselves affect the cerebral cortex and warn us that we are begin-

ning to be annoyed. The original stimulus itself may
also be continuing to solicit our emotions. If the will,
which could have distracted our attention to other
things, gives in to anger, we shall retain the concrete
judgment, "I, They, It." This judgment will become
stronger and more prolonged and will prepare us
for attack or some other reaction.

The reaction may be wholly unrestrained, in which
case the hypothalamus will develop an *animal wrath*
or unrestrained anger with primitive animal reactions. Or perhaps, faced with social conventions or
fear of reprisals, we shall be content with a restrained
attack, that is to say, with a corroding *impatience*
which will be accompanied by threats, or by acts
which annoy our adversary, or by a feeling of disgust
or sadness. Or, finally, we may resolve to postpone
the attack, on which occasion we conceive *hatred* or
"bottled wrath" together with tension and prolonged
inner disturbances.

In all of these three states the organism calls all its
reserves into battle: the overexcited autonomic nervous system, the adrenalin which flows in the bloodstream and activates all the organs, the pituitary
gland which liberates the hormone ACTH. This latter stimulates the suprarenal glands where there are
manufactured what we might call the Atomic Bombs
of the organism, i.e., the groups of hormones which
affect mineral metabolism, gluco-metabolism, and
androgen. All these help to produce a revolution or
overexcitation which is more sustained than that of
the nervous system, but which liberates an enormous
amount of energy as if for use in an emergency.

Moreover, the medulla of the suprarenal glands
produces adrenalin which then stimulates even more

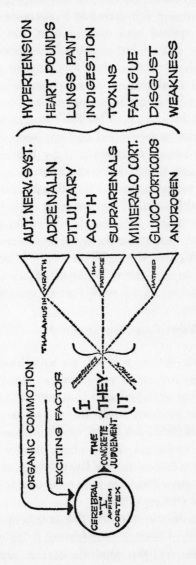

the hypothalamus and the pituitary gland. Then we begin to feel the effects of hypertension in the circulatory system and musculature, the heart pounds, and the lungs labor as if to obtain more oxygen. The stomach contracts, thus stopping or disturbing the process of digestion. The whole organism becomes poisoned if anger is prolonged, and then fatigue and disgust invade us. After the emotion has passed, our resistance is weakened and we become depressed at feeling ourselves conquered by the emotion. Sometimes, too, there may come upon us an unholy joy at seeing an adversary suffer. But all these evils can be avoided by controlling the concrete judgment and by making anger subordinate to reason rather than to passion. Otherwise there are results such as in a New Orleans clinic where 76 per cent of the patients were found to be there because of anger, hatred, or impatience, mixed with fear or anxiety.

II. Victorious Development

When the signals of an emotional disturbance come to the cerebral cortex, we notice that we are becoming annoyed and that our organism is beginning to prepare itself for attack or defense. The stimulus itself, the injury or the memory of one, may still be exciting us also. Then, instead of letting ourselves be dominated by the emotion, if we order that it be controlled, the free will can follow either or both of two procedures.

First, it can modify the concrete judgment, "I, They, It," either by weakening it through a distraction or, better, annihilating it by a contrary judgment.

Secondly, it can order the contrary internal attitude of love and sympathy and the external expression of this on the face, in the tone of voice, and in muscular activity.

1. Control by means of distraction

"Every morning," says the Doctor of Gentleness, St. Francis de Sales, "prepare your soul for a tranquil day." When you are at peace, foster this advantageous state for the sake of your own advancement. Continually exercise yourself in acts of goodness and gentleness. If something bothers you, do not be disturbed or resist it. But when it comes, humble yourself graciously in the presence of God and try to put your soul into a tranquil state. Say, "Yes, I stumbled there; I must be more careful." Do this always, however often you fail. Wait, have patience, gather your forces and you will win the spirit of peace and gentleness.

We have often heard this advice given: "Calm down, don't answer, control yourself, have patience." It would be more effective if, instead of wanting to remove the feeling (which is an effect of ideas), we were to remove or modify the ideas which cause it. When another insults you or his conduct disgusts you, instead of thinking about the injustice or grossness of his behavior, concentrate your attention on something else—objects or colors before you, or the sound waves coming at you from all directions, or (if you are a psychologist) in observing his waste of energy, his attitudes and reactions. You would then feel hardly any commotion.

2. *Control by means of the contrary idea*

(1) Discover which of the three, "I, They, It" predominates in you and formulate the contrary of it.

(2) To the thought of pride or fear which the emotion arouses, e.g., "I do not deserve this treatment," oppose the following: "I am a man like others, with limitations, defects and transgressions which would deserve a greater punishment."

Instead of the idea that "They are unjust or cruel," insist on what experience teaches, namely that "Everyone has lesser defects and greater virtues than we tend to admit when we are angry." Or, "They must have done that without thinking of what they were doing, or at least there was no bad will there." Jesus Christ on the Cross used this means when He asked pardon for those who crucified and insulted Him, saying that their guilt was less because "they know not what they do."

(3) If you are a spiritual man, a Christian with a living faith, reflect that an insult is what you deserve because of your sins. Think that it is a great opportunity offered you by God to gain by a minute's patience and humiliation "an eternal reward of glory."

A Sister of Charity was once begging alms for her orphans. "An alms?" answered an anticlerical, "To support you in idleness and help enslave those kids? This is what you need." And he struck her. The Sister thought for a moment about her sins and replied without a change of countenance, "That was for me, sir. Now, something for my orphans." The man's anger vanished; he asked her pardon and gave her a substantial donation.

If the mere presence of that good person for whom you have an aversion draws a curl to your lip and brings you a thousand sharp thoughts and words, do a bit of spiritual gymnastics and meditate on his virtues. See in him "Jesus Christ disguised in his defects," who draws near to you that you may smile on Him, love Him, speak to Him, and serve Him with greater merit. Our Divine Master said, "As long as you did it for one of these, the least of my brethren, you did it for Me."

(4) Finally, the event itself, the "It," is not too unbearable nor too dangerous. If it deprives us of some earthly good, or convenience, or comfort, yet this and all the goods of the world are no more than an insignificant speck of dust in comparison with the everlasting goods which are prepared as the reward of our suffering. "Although it be encircled with thorns, it is a diamond for heaven." Injury or insult is an incendiary explosion which can be triggered and detonated only by our thoughts of protest. (At the end of Chapter XIV you will find some examples of thoughts for changing sorrow into joy.)

3. Control by means of the contrary feeling

We must try to substitute feelings of joy, peace, and sympathy for the feeling of disgust, perturbation, or antipathy which our emotions would tend to arouse in us. Above all we must digest inevitable suffering by accepting it fully, if we wish it not to go on poisoning us. We must treat persons *as if* they were very congenial and sympathetic. We must try to understand and value their virtues and excuse their defects. We must use a tone of respectful affection, pay them deference and do them services, pray and sacrifice for them. A month of this treatment will be enough to make us congenial and sympathetic ourselves. For knowing how to think well of others and how to smile on them is the secret of multiplying friends.

Bandits once attacked the house of a colleague of mine in China. He received their chiefs with all courtesy and kindness, just as he would orderly and more advanced people. He invited them to tea, candy and cigarettes in his reception room. When he brought them to the door, they met others of the bandits making off with the missionary's mules. The chiefs ordered them returned and went away without doing any harm whatever.

4. Control by means of the contrary expression

We should also use the method which is more physiological. Our voice, breathing, eyes and muscles should be given an expression contrary to that which anger would impose upon us. We should either remain silent or at least speak deliberately, quietly, and pleasantly. If a cry of hatred or impatience is about to escape through your mouth, breathe deeply two or three times and release the air slowly, and you will extinguish it. Keep the muscles of arms and hands, mouth and face loose and relaxed. Above all make sure that a smile gives the eyes a kindly, gentle expression. And at the same time keep your thoughts on something pleasant.

After one of my lectures in Rio de Janeiro a lady came up to tell me about her troubles, her bad temper and that of her husband. "My home is a hell," she said. "We are always quarreling, although we pass for good Christians, and even devout ones." I advised that she go look at herself in a mirror and practice smiling with her eyes. "When you have learned how to make this deep and open smile, and when you know that your husband is returning home, make an act of Faith: 'Here comes Jesus Christ disguised in the defects of my husband. He is coming so that I may smile at Him, love Him, and serve Him.'" A month later she came back to thank me for the advice; her home had been transformed. They were happy. She had modified the thought and the external expression of anger.

XII

Fear

Could we succeed in banishing exaggerated insecurity and fear from the earth, we would double the health and happiness of the human race.

As children, says Fosdick, we feared only two things: falling down and loud noises. After passing through the fears of childhood, experience teaches us that many fears are groundless. And we protect ourselves against unreasonable fears. Yet oftentimes the environment and our imagination lead us to see dangers where there are really none. Or they may magnify our fears a hundredfold.

Strong impressions of terror or lively bouts of anxiety and fear, whether they come from conversation, or from a vivid imagination, or the movies, leave something like a residue or sedimentation in the subconscious. This residue is a tendency toward insecurity or a feeling of anxiety. And when this feeling invades an idle mind, it tends to fill it with anxiety images, provoking organic alterations such as physical inhibitions, trembling, contraction of the blood vessels, pallor, panting for breath, palpitations, and so forth. Fear is a monster which dwells in the caverns of the subconscious. The more vague and confused it is, the more it afflicts us. We should drag it out from its hidden lair, look at it face to face, and then we shall destroy it.

Degrees of Fear

We said in the first part that the idea or apprehension of "danger," whether real or imaginary, is the cause of fear. Fear and its consequent inhibitions keep on increasing in proportion to the magnitude of the danger, its proximity, and the difficulty of avoiding it. So at the mere possibility of a misfortune or because of an imagined inability to cope with it, our physical movements and our very speech lose their spontaneity. When we merely walk out in front of a large audience, all of whom have their eyes on us, very few of us will even walk naturally. If our lack of confidence turns into alarm at a really probable or great danger, the unity of our wishing, thinking, and acting is broken, and even our muscles tremble. We are literally "shaken up" and if the serious danger or misfortune seems to be *inevitable*, then anxiety tends to destroy all control of movements, ideas and emotions. Even the memory can be inhibited, as when timid students take examinations.

Finally, if the fear goes a step further and the

danger seems to be imminent, serious and inevitable, panic can take hold of us and bring anarchy into our thoughts, feelings, and actions. Paralysis of all our powers may follow if the fear is extremely great. An example of this is the confusion and witless panic that often come with an earthquake or a fire in a theater.

HOW TO CONTROL FEAR

Fear is the emotion most difficult to control because often we do not know what we fear or why we are afraid, as in cases of anxiety, phobias, or groundless fears. The motive is often unconscious or may be transferred from its real cause to some accompanying circumstance. Or we may be unconsciously repressing some natural reaction which might humiliate us, we think, if seen.

Instead, we give it expression in "symbolic" fears which we recognize as groundless, but which we do not know how to control. In such cases a deeper exploration of the subconscious is indicated, an investigation of the abnormality and the circumstances which first accompanied it. Discovering these, we may easier control a transferred fear.

If the fear is *conscious*, we may take the following steps to conquer it:

1. Before all else, act. Fear already tends to inhibit our activities. So we must not assist it by remaining inactive but, on the contrary, conquer it by acting. A North Pole explorer owes his rescue to such a procedure. Lost on the endless ice, he could not find his camp. Instead of worrying about it, he began to heap up piles of snow and ice at regular intervals.

These helped him to make calculations through which he eventually rediscovered his camp.

2. *Make them concrete.* We must illuminate those dark caverns. Answer these questions in writing and in detail: "Just what am I afraid of? And why?" When fear or anxiety is made concrete and viewed objectively, it is destroyed.

3. *Reason about them.* "What probabilities are there that this [the thing I fear] will really happen? And even if it does happen, will it really be as disastrous as I fear?"

4. *Face up to them.* "Even supposing that this happens, what then? So what? Are there not others who have gone through similar crises? Haven't they gone on living and become happy? And even if I have to die, so what? Then can't I begin to be happier in eternity?"

When we imagine the worst possible natural evil that could happen to us and sincerely accept it and so find a human or divine solution for it, we shall be victorious over exaggerated fear.

5. Avoid the exciting factors, or rather the alarming ideas which these stimuli arouse in us. Distract your attention from them by means of concentrating it upon conscious sensations or by deliberately following out a favorite train of thought or, even better,—

6. Deliberately affirm *contrary judgments,* e.g., "There is no special danger. The probability that this will happen is very small. Even if it does happen, the disadvantage would be insignificant, or at least

there would come with it several advantages which would far counterbalance it."

7. Deliberately foster *contrary feelings,* e.g., of courage, or security. This is done by the same means by which fear betrayed us, i.e., by intense acts of courage, by vivid remembrances of peaceful moments or places, by actually saying something with a tone of courage or security in the voice.

8. Associate this reliving of past peaceful moments with the circumstances which had been producing anxiety in you. Imagine that you are in control of the situation and that you are speaking in a masterful tone of voice such as in the case of the young man with the pills or the patient with the locust [Chapter V].

In a Brazilian seminary I met a stammerer who was afraid that he would be unable to go on to the priesthood because of this defect. Face to face with the Rector of the seminary he could not speak two consecutive words. The same thing would happen when with certain of his companions and in certain classes. On the contrary he spoke well whenever he had learned something by memory. Hence it was the feeling of anxiety which was inhibiting his vocal muscles. He was afraid that the Rector would declare him unsuitable for the priesthood. But I helped him to remove this fear by showing him that he could cure himself if he would implant the contrary feelings in his subconscious by the means indicated above. And so I had him link these feelings to the experience which had terrified him most. I had him imagine and then actually say, "I am going to see Father Rector . . . I greet him . . . And all is serene. I am completely at peace and am master of the situation." At first he spoke the last phrase with the same descriptive tone as the first. But I had him repeat it after me with a tone of security. On doing it with all the courage and force of which he was capable, I felt that he was transformed. Three days later the Rector came to thank me for the good done to his seminarians, and he particularly mentioned that the stammerer had been cured.

9. *In cases of muscular constriction.* By this I mean a latent state of insecurity or anxiety due to strong and prolonged tension in the intercostal muscles. This prevents the quiet easy expansion of the chest which is normal when we are secure or in good spirits. Instead, we would then tend to assume a posture characteristic of timidity or depression. But, since there appear to be no mental or emotional causes of fear, we should try to loosen these muscles by adequate gymnastic exercises, a more correct posture, or massage.

10. Assume the opposite facial expression: not the wide open, staring eyes which are a sign of fear, but rather a look that is secure and mild. Keep the voice deep and firm; let it rely on the outgoing air current and not on forcing the throat muscles. Maintain a respiration that is deeper or slower. To do this, instead of concentrating on expanding the lungs, try to expand the nasal passages and keep them well opened.

HOW TO CONTROL SCRUPLES

The obsessing insecurity of scruples can find expression in profane matters, as in the case of one who goes out of his house and is worried whether he put out the lights, turned off the faucet, or locked the door. This kind of obsession also, and frequently, finds expression in religious or moral affairs. A religious scruple is a torturing but unfounded fear of sinning or having sinned. It is an error or anguishing doubt caused by a strong fear which inhibits or disturbs the reason. Scruples are the source of anxiety or sadness, of many organic ailments, bashfulness, and many personality disturbances. If not controlled in time, scruples can become the occasion of despair, moral relapses, and even moral perversion.

The predisposing causes of scruples are the same as those indicated above for exaggerated impressionability or exaggerated emotions in general, such as organic weakness and nervous exhaustion. Another cause is a temperament that tends to look upon the negative side of things. Or it may be one or more of the following: a residue of insecurity because of not having taken action against previous unreasonable fears; an uncontrolled and exaggerated imagination; an excessively strict education; much dealing with scrupulous people; an anxious desire for excessive certitude; or fear of responsibility. A scruple may also be a temptation of the devil. When it is very prolonged, it is almost always an indication of psychoneurosis and sometimes of psychosis. In other words, a scruple can be one of many symptoms of mental illness, but of itself it does not indicate an evil moral life or lack of faith.

REMEDIES FOR SCRUPLES

1. Before all else make sure that it is really a scruple and not merely ignorance or a passing test prompted by God. This judgment should be made by the director or advisor and not by the person himself.

2. Then admit what is scientifically proven, that is, that scruples are a mental and not a moral illness. To convince yourself of this, read over the symptoms which appear on the outline diagram in Chapter II. The scrupulous person will find that he has more than one of these symptoms. He should recall what we said about the "degrees of fear." Whenever the fear is great (and there is no greater fear than that caused by the idea of "eternal damnation"), this not only inhibits and disturbs his muscles, but also his mind and feelings. The emotion of fear is so disturbing to the scrupulous person that it makes him see danger where there is none, or see grave sin where there is only an imperfection or a venial fault.

3. Fight the battle on the proper terrain. Do not pretend to destroy this mental *and natural* enemy with means that are spiritual or supernatural such as absolution. What should we say to someone who comes up to a priest and keeps saying, "Father save me. I have such a toothache I know I am going to hell." The answer should be: "Go see a dentist, but do not think you are lost because of a reason like that." The scrupulous person must be told something similar. "Do not give an eternal dimension to what is only an emotional disturbance."

4. Recognize, then, that emotion *disturbs the judgment* so much that it makes one see what does not exist. This often happens when timid persons think they see apparitions at night. They forget it when

they discover that the phantasm, or appearance, is really something that they know very well. But they run away in terror if the fear gets control of them. Once upon a time there was a blind man, led along by a guide, who all of a sudden stopped and said, "I can't go another step; I *see* a deep pit in front of me." Of course, being blind, he could not see what was really not there, but he had something in his imagination. Something like this happens in the case of the scrupulous man when, despite his confessor's judgment, he sees sin and sacrilege in receiving Communion. We should insist that he receive Communion, but, instead of losing time examining his conscience over and over again and weighing the "sacrilege" that he thinks he sees, he should repeat acts of love and confidence. Such faith and obedience, which relinguish one's own judgment for God's sake, are heroic. And each such act of love itself gives or increases grace.

5. Whoever had a clock or thermometer out of order would be advised by everyone not to be guided by it, but to follow normal clocks or thermometers. So, God gives a right to the scrupulous person not to be guided or changed by what his disturbed conscience tells him, but by what his director tells him. More than this, his Heavenly Father asks him to use this right, to lay aside for a time his subjective judgment, and to remain at peace.

6. When the scruple is concerned with one's past life, even despite a series of general confessions; when a person thinks that he has forgotten or has not confessed well, or that his confessors have not understood him, he should remember that by means

194]ACHIEVINGPEACEOFHEART

of indirect absolution all his sins have already been forgiven on the day on which he made a confession with good will. The obligation of making known forgotten sins in a subsequent confession pertains only to those which are certainly mortal, certainly committed, and certainly omitted from confession. And even this obligation ceases for a scrupulous person.

7. Many confuse the concepts of perfect confession and good confession. An absolutely perfect confession could be made only by God who knows perfectly the responsibility of every act. We can all make at least a good confession, for this demands only good will on our part. Many scrupulous people could hardly do any more than this because of the blocks in their minds and their disturbed emotions. They should realize, then, that in such a good confession absolution directly pertains to the sins of which they accuse themselves, and indirectly pertains to those which they have forgotten or those of which they did not accuse themselves perfectly, although they acted with good will at the time of the confession.

More than this, when their nervousness and confused ideas about the examination of conscience and confession itself begin to torture them, we must remember what moral theology teaches us, that the integrity of confession would tend to bring them a serious psychical damage. At such times, with their confessor's approval, they may content themselves with a general accusation or merely ask for absolution, renewing their contrition for all their past sins.

8. In the case of scrupulous people who are obsessed with doubts concerning internal acts, such as their thoughts, desires, intentions, feelings, sorrow, or purpose of amendment, they should be forbidden not only to accuse themselves, but even to examine themselves in this regard. For if it is difficult for all of us to measure our responsibility for such internal acts, for the scrupulous person it is impossible. The scrupulous person is often concerned about his "thoughts." So he must be told that thoughts, of themselves, are not sins. To be sinful the thought, for instance, of a forbidden pleasure would have to be deliberately *chosen by the will*. And one would have to want the thought with the intention of gaining the forbidden pleasure, relishing the thought somewhat as one who chews a caramel.

9. Since the scrupulous person is scarcely living at all in the present and does not take exact account of what he sees and hears but is always wrapped up in his subjective thoughts, he should work to increase his conscious life with voluntary sensations by "living in the present" or by practicing the "Do what you are doing." (See Chapter IV.)

10. He should also re-educate his power of concentration by accustoming himself to think about only one thing at a time. The scrupulous man does not know how to detach himself from his obsession whenever he is studying, conversing, or walking.

11. Above all, he should strengthen his will by repeated acts of decision and by assuming responsibilities. These activities have in his case been almost

extinguished. To this end the director should not always take upon himself the responsibility for decisions, but, little by little, should bring it about that the person suffering from scruples take this responsibility upon himself.

After a lecture a lady came to see me. She had been suffering for seventeen years from persistent scruples. These had stolen away all her peace and joy. She could not go to Communion unless confession had immediately preceded it. Even then she went in fear and trembling. She seemed quite discouraged and in a decline. I proved to her that her illness was not moral but psychic. I managed to convince her that she had nothing to fear for her soul, but that her health was in danger. I explained that the working of a scruple was not intellectual but emotional. For example, there were one or more frightful experiences or thoughts establishing this feeling in the unconscious. From this unconscious level they bothered her by arousing fear of sin, either when similar images or happenings occurred or when she had similar depressing feelings.

I explained to her the conditions for mortal sin: full consciousness and a deliberate act of the will in a serious matter. These conditions were, of course, not verified in her case. By thus eliminating the root of fear she could promise herself that in the future she would not fear the scruple but discredit it. She would substitute a conscious sensation for it whenever it arose. By means of conscious acts, each time repeated more frequently, she began to come out of her merely subjective world and live in the objective order. She was cured by the time she had come for two interviews. When I saw her again six months later, she was healthy, joyful and happy. The scruples returned only once, during a mental crisis occasioned by the death of her father. But she mastered them in a very short time.

12. He should exact of himself blind obedience to his director, an obedience which is founded upon supernatural faith. He should recognize that he is blind, that he needs a guide, and that for the time being he has a right not to be guided by or make changes in accordance with what his disturbed conscience tells him. He should follow what his director says to do. And in moments of doubt he must adhere to what has been determined or resolved upon at a more tranquil time or with the director's aid.

13. He should not be moved by doubts or a "perhaps," but only by evidence, and he should faithfully observe the following three rules:

a) Never to accuse himself of doubts or temptations concerning the matter about which (his director has advised him) he is scrupulous.

b) Not to review or talk about his past confessions or sins of his past life.

c) While going about his everyday business, not to give any importance to sudden doubts.

He must accept the fact that his illness has been derived from throwing himself into action while in a state of doubt, and that it is an illness which is valuable experience for him because it helps him to get control of his anxiety and get closer to a normal state. He must accept the fact that everytime he tries to obtain any momentary alleviation of his trouble by means of giving in to his tendency to doubt, such an occasion will be a prologue to greater troubles.

14. He should be content with human security about salvation or the state of grace. He should not desire to have the kind of security or certitude proper to God's knowledge or that of men who are in heaven (the kind that excludes all possibility of the opposite). Thus he will help to bring about that state of confidence which is so pleasing to God.

15. He should increase this confidence by repeated concrete acts, even if the effort to overcome the contrary feeling calls for heroism on his part.

16. He should fight against the unconscious feeling of fear or doubt which is the remote root of scruples. He should frequently repeat thoughts, sentences and acts of courage and confidence.

Recall the case of St. Francis de Sales for whom an intense and prolonged expression of love was the adequate counterweight and cure for a tendency to scrupulosity.

17. Change the negative attitude of a person who fears and trembles at sin and personal responsibility for a different, positive attitude which concentrates on and examines how he might have pleased God more, aided his neighbor more effectively, or practiced virtue in a better way. He should shift the direction of his thoughts and self-examination from sins to the virtues.

18. Finally, he should relax the tensions in his muscles and practice breathing more slowly, rhyth-

mically, and deeply. Especially should he practice
relaxation of eyes and forehead. He should wear a
smile on his face like one who knows that his fears
were exaggerated and due to an illness rather than
being any real danger to his soul.

What begins as timidity or cowardice can degenerate into a feeling of inferiority or an "inferiority
complex." This may be due to there having been
little or no expression of security or of one's own
personality during infancy or adolescence. Perhaps
his education was excessively protective and warded
off from him every exposure to difficulty or danger.
This would likely result in an inability to overcome
difficulty or danger. Or perhaps other people always
made the decisions for him, and he never became
accustomed to assuming responsibility himself. Or
it may have been due to a frequent experience of
fear which was not counteracted at once by positive
thoughts. Then the fear remained at a subconscious
level in the same manner as insecurity or a tendency
to be upset (like one who is easily "shaken up" or
easily "thrown off balance").

Or all this may come from a *false concept of
inferiority* because of some past failure, the importance and consequences of which his wounded self-
love multiplies a hundredfold. Or his timidity may
be grounded upon some *real* defect or a *real* inca-
pacity in one particular field, which his imagination
extends to other areas while hiding away his real
talents and good qualities.

It may even be due to an *excessive ambition* or to

the kind of depression that results from seeking unrealistic goals. Or he may be a man seeking merely human success without giving importance to success in the eyes of God. In other words, whoever in all his actions seeks and delights in realizing the will of God, the ideal of Infinite Wisdom, by this alone can feel full satisfaction even though human success fails him. For God's highest plans may include human failure without impeding His glory. God obtains what He desires not by our action but through our sanctification, humiliation or other supernatural means.

Sometimes this feeling of inferiority may come from an *irrational panic about "what they will say"* or fear of ridicule. Timidity is in direct proportion to our desire of not being criticized. Hence, the capacity to laugh at oneself and at everything laughable counteracts timidity. Laughter is the secret of good humor, a fountain of health, and a condition of our acceptance in society.

A sense of inferiority is sometimes the result of *comparing oneself to others.* This is especially liable to happen if a person is involved with others who are better prepared or highly talented. In such a situation think of the fact that everyone has his own good qualities and aptitudes from God and that he will give an account of them to God. Remember that the man who received ten talents and gained ten others was not more highly praised than the man who received one talent and gained one more. You must develop your own personality—"Be yourself!"—and not try to be a "rubber stamp" of anyone else. The grandeur of man is not in physical appearance but

in moral value. Oftentimes a noble and heroic soul
is disguised in a sick or deformed body.

The Extent of This Evil

An investigation of 270 students in a North American university found 240 of them with feelings of
frustration or deficiency, physical inability, a not
very sympathetic presence, conflicting loves, little
aptitude for study or social life, and remorse.

There are students with brilliant compositions in
a written examination whom fear of the examiners
will disturb and make awkward in an oral examination. Unexperienced orators and poets, who have
prepared magnificent compositions, at sight of an
exacting audience will begin to tremble. They will
grow pale, stutter and even forget what they have
learned or prepared. Too severe criticism had, after
their first trials, cut their wings for life. There are
well trained men who after a failure in business or
at one job think themselves unsuited for new ven-
tures. And there are people who converse pleasantly
and act courteously who one day are caught ill prepared. We see them grow mute, flush when they
have to participate in a social event and finally
change into misanthropic solitaries. Typists, pianists,
children and young people who are extraordinarily
gifted in private or within their family circle often
seem nonentities in the presence of other people.

This timidity must not be confused with humility,
for it sometimes arises from pride. It causes its
victim no little suffering from blushing, trembling, palpitations and stammering. These symptoms
appear and disappear without apparent cause. They

can even bring on lasting phobias or a mental inhibition. When they border on an emotional shock, they weaken or paralyze the muscles. Humility is not depressing. It is truth and raises one up toward God and confidence in Him. Timidity frequently increases or is caused by it.

You must war against so widespread an evil. Above all, do not cause such a feeling in children or youths by continually reminding them of and exaggerating their defects. They must, on the contrary, be encouraged and shown their possibilities for progress. Do not, even as a joke, give a child terror of ghosts, the dead, darkness or animals. This will probably remain active in his subconscious even after he has grown up. On the contrary, you must encourage and show them how to make progress. Manage things so that they do triumph in some matter; get them to be outstanding in something. Little by little get them to face up to difficulties and conquer them. Teach them to use their liberty well, to undertake tasks that are gradually more difficult, to make decisions and assume responsibilities for themselves. And when they fail or fear failure, help them to overcome even this by convincing them that they should not be discouraged but should profit from their failure (or fear of failure), learn how to get on their feet again, and so develop even greater strength.

Cure

If you find this timidity in yourself, calmly examine the thoughts and motives which cause it. Remove exaggerated deductions from your subconsciousness and have trust in yourself. Make an examination of your timidity in writing and show this to your director or mental adviser. You know that there is no reason for being a coward, that all men are equal, that you are superior to most in your own specialty, that there are many mediocre people, that geniuses know how to cover up their deficiencies and show their good qualities. Soak yourself in these ideas. Boil them down into suggestive formulas and frequently repeat them, especially when signs of timidity appear.

With such convictions and suggestions attack the emotional difficulties. Begin with the easier ones. Take courage at every victory, often repeating, "I am going to win out," "Each time I have more courage," and so forth. Never use negative formulas or conjure up the memory of phobias or symptoms which disturb you. If you say, for instance, "I am not going to blush," "I won't tremble," "I won't stammer," you will produce the very effect you wish to avoid.

Timid people usually remember their failures and easily forget their triumphs. To modify this negative memory, they should not think voluntarily about any past failure. On the contrary, they should note down their daily successes and those of the past. In moments of discouragement they will profit from reading over these notes.

There is also a *supernatural* remedy to use. Let them stir up their faith in God who appreciates us, loves us, and can help us. Draw the conclusion from this: "Humble, yes; timid, no." For "I can do all things in Him who strengthens me." We should accept our limitations, then, for we are all clay as well as spirit. In Adam we have all fallen, but Christ has raised us up; He calls us and we are in truth "adopted children of God."

Blushing and Embarrassment

A very common manifestation of a feeling of inferiority is the habit of blushing and the obvious embarrassment which accompanies it. For this reason we should never make fun of those who blush easily. Suffering is always something sacred and should be respected even when it is subjective in origin. Sometimes it can have very deep roots in wounded self-love, something we did not—or do not—want to accept or admit. The aid of a specialist will then be very useful in discovering and overcoming such a deep-rooted wish. In ordinary cases we should not give importance to so natural and common a phenomenon. For it only indicates modesty and virtue (bad people do not blush). Go ahead *as if* this did not matter to you and take a greater part in the conversation. Pay more attention to what is being said or done. Let this attention fill the field of your consciousness. With no attention given them, the illusions suggested by timidity and caused by blushing will disappear.

One young teacher who blushed and sweated before his students was greatly impressed and cured by the following reasoning process. "If in spite of feeling myself beginning to blush, I go on firmly and energetically without worrying about it, then I am not only not inferior to others, but greater and stronger than all of them. For almost anyone else would act like a coward in these circumstances."

The means of conquering fear or timidity which have been explained above, especially those which give support to one's personality, are also advisable as a cure for unreasonable blushing. In particular one might try to reproduce in his mind the circumstances in which he blushed without cause. Let him imagine these vividly and think of himself as serene, then speak about them, using a tone of voice of absolute security.

One day Father Laburu[1] was asked to interview a young man, 25 years old, who blushed in the presence of anyone whomsoever. Father Laburu discovered that this had been going on since the young man was eleven years old. One day he had done something wrong on the way to school. The teacher called upon him to recite, and at once he blushed. Asked why he blushed so violently, he lied. This bothered him so much that on the following day he blushed again while reciting. Then it started to happen while speaking to his father and later with other persons, too. Father Laburu discovered the cause for him and had him reproduce in his imagination the original circumstances which made such a strong impression on him. He had him recite after him, and with the same controlled tone of voice, "I am in front of my father and feel calm, completely secure, and happy." As soon as he succeeded in pronouncing these words with a tone of security, he felt transformed.

For a bodily treatment you are recommended any tonic or strengthener of the nervous system, breath-

---

[1] *Psicologia Medica*, by Father Laburu, S.J., Montevideo: Mosca Hnos, 1945 (lectures delivered in the University of Buenos Aires).

ing exercises, sports or any moderate physical exercise. Practice sureness of gaze, not that you should seem to be staring or boldly provocative, or trying to pierce behind a companion's eyes. But practice a gaze which looks easily and dignifiedly at a point between another person's eyes. If you have photophobia (that is, if light bothers you) keep your back to the source of the light or use tinted glasses.

Superiors or directors who treat with timid people will do well not to look at their eyes or forehead or even sit directly in front of them, but toward the side. Thus the timid will be less bashful and more confident. Nor should they be required before special training to perform acts of self-conquest in which a great objective difficulty comes more from timidity or phobias than pride or a lack of mortification.

Orators who experience their breath growing shorter or being choked off just before stepping up onto the speaking platform should breathe deeply for five or ten seconds, emptying their lungs of used air. At the subsequent automatic filling of their lungs with pure air they will begin to speak with a sure voice and will conquer their timidity.

The Supernatural Remedy

For those who have faith the great remedy is a concrete and heroic confidence in God who can and will aid us. For He commands us "not to fear," not even "those who can kill the body." Their remedy is also confident and persevering prayer which obtains whatever it asks for. "The more you ask for when you pray, believe that you will receive it and it shall be given to you." Here as elsewhere we must avoid timidity. We must not make the future present, for where the future is made present it is disfigured. The only time that exists is now. The past did exist, but does no longer; the future may exist, but does not yet. The only two important times, as Catholics acknowledge in the *Hail Mary,* are "now and at the hour of our death."

VALUES TO THINK ABOUT

"Per angusta ad augusta," said the ancient Romans. In other words, the road to grandeur leads through difficulties.

"Patientia opus perfectum habet." In other words, patience is the secret of perfection. Patience will every day bring me some improvement and some useful experience.

A bent blade of grass is not dead, but can raise itself up anew.

There is no night so dark but that some lamp is shining.

Whatever does not conquer me makes me stronger. Only a dead fish drifts downstream without being able to swim against the current.

Each day we can learn to see better the face of suffering and convert it into joy. Each day I can better see the good side of things and learn how to use them better for a good purpose.

No failure should cause me to lose a joyful and optimistic hope for the eventual success of our undertakings.

If I learn how to profit from the lesson, even defeat will be transformed into strength.

Just as knowing how to fall correctly is necessary for certain sports, so for victory in life we must know

how to win even when we are beaten. We must
learn how to fall without discouragement, to lose
without irritation, to fail without despair, to suffer
without sadness.

I can do all things in Him who strengthens me.

If God be with us, who shall stand against us? If
the Almighty is with me, whom shall I fear?

OUTLINE DIAGRAM

※⊃•⊂※

How to Control Feelings

IN GENERAL
- A chaotic force: direct it.
- Do not be governed by likes or dislikes, but by reason.
- Govern them
  - by lessening their exaggerations
  - making no change merely on their account
  - thinking about the opposite
  - working against the feeling.
- Their release
  - useful—in affective conflicts, noble affections
  - useless—impulsive confidences
  - harmful—from passion

IN PARTICULAR
- Dominate anger
  - controlling thoughts
  - thinking about something else, the opposite
  - working "as if . . ."
- **FEELING OF INFERIORITY**
  - Causes
    - failures, defects, criticisms
    - fear of "what they will say"
  - Effects
    - suffering, apprehensive fear, embarrassment (blushing), paralysis, irritation
  - Remedies
    - preventive
      - not to exaggerate faults
      - not to instill vain fears
    - curative
      - examine the root cause and its path
      - conviction and suggestion of courage
      - attack difficulties by degrees
  - Supernatural remedies
    - confidence
    - prayer

XIII

Sadness

THE EMOTION OF SADNESS is due to the idea of *failure* in an action or enterprise, the idea of *frustration* of some desire or hope, or frustration in life itself, the idea of *lack* or *loss* of a good, or the idea of a *present evil* which we synthesize in the word "suffering." It will be the more acute and penetrating as the loss is greater or seems greater, and all the more paralyzing as the remedy seems far away. It will be a negative sadness or despair if the three concepts of *loss*, *total* loss, and *irreparable* loss are joined together. Hence no sadness can be greater than that which accompanies the thought of hell, where the loss is evidently infinite and without remedy for all eternity.

There are specific harms resulting from sadness in addition to the usual effects of all depressive emotions, e.g., fatigue, hypertension, arthritis, asthma, and digestive and circulatory disturbances. In two words, sadness "slows down and paralyzes." Sadness slows down all one's vitality, efficiency, health, nutritional processes, etc., and sometimes paralyzes them. If there is exaggeration in the idea of loss, this can become obsessing and prevent us from attending to other things, especially when it is also joined to an emotion of fear or disgust.

These effects may also extend to one's spiritual and social life. To serve God with sadness while He is heaping benefits upon us is to dishonor and displease Him. Boredom and tepidity will soon follow. A life of virtue will seem intolerable, and an illusory and harmful compensation may be sought for in luxury. Our neighbor, too, is annoyed by our sad eyes, for these emit rays of sadness and tell him that he does not please us.

Predisposing Causes

The *organic* cause of this emotion or, better, the temperamental predisposition to hold onto sad thoughts and feelings can have its origin in general illness or a specific infirmity, especially in one connected with the stomach or liver. It may also come from prolonged fatigue, or the chronic tiredness of elderly people.

The predisposing *psychical* causes are manifold.

(1) *Perfectionism.* When we build up for ourselves a utopian ideal which goes beyond our own capacity or expects too much from others, we become "perfectionists." We may make our happiness depend upon *excessive* demands for personal attentions, comforts, entertainment, success, and so forth. Then the idea of frustration in not having these demands satisfied will always be plaguing us. We should remedy this by accepting our limitations and not aiming at or hoping for so very much satisfaction, so many attentions from others, or so many personal triumphs for ourselves. In brief, we should not set the price of happiness so high.

*   (2) *Negativism.* This is often the result of a child-hood experience in which our elders kept harping on our defects and the defects of others. As children, then, we did not learn how to discover the good in ourselves or others. Or perhaps we ourselves are responsible for developing a negative and pessimistic attitude because of a habit of recalling to mind our difficulties and personal defects, forgetting the victories and joys of life. In such cases, instead of developing a positive and optimistic tendency, the master-idea of our life becomes the idea of loss or failure.

The pessimist will say about a rose: "Too bad it has thorns." An optimist, on the other hand, will see the thorns and say, "It's wonderful that thorns can accompany so beautiful a flower." The pessimist is sad at thinking that one day is surrounded by two nights; the optimist is joyful at expecting two days with one night. The former sees that a bottle is half empty; to the latter it is still half full.

(3) *Hysterical egoism.* This type wants to seem to be a "victim" so that others will take pity on him. He will talk about and exaggerate his ills and sadness as a "bid" to attract attention.

(4) A predisposition to sadness. *Hunger for appreciation is never sated.* Sometimes in childhood we experience a kind of anxiety for affection and, when we do not get it, we feel that our rights have been violated. Sometimes in later life we feel that we have been frustrated or unsuccessful in love, and this vacuum of affection can continue for the rest of one's life and easily lead to a chronic state of sadness. One example: a missionary whom I knew in

the Far East often used to experience a feeling of
frustration despite his sacrifices and generosity with
God and souls. He became so sad that he began to
doubt whether he had a true vocation. I asked him
one question: "Were you treated affectionately as a
child?" He lowered his eyes and answered, "I never
knew my mother, and my father never showed us
any affection." Then I hinted that this affective
vacuum could explain his present state and in no
way indicated a lack of vocation. At this he felt
greatly relieved. His spirits rose and he set out to
compensate for that defect by deliberately taking
means to feel the infinite love of God for him and
making a return of his own love to God. He also
expressed this in work for the service of his neighbor
—with whom Christ wished to identify Himself.

The hunger for affection may come from an opposite source if, for instance, as children, we were
treated with so much indulgence that this became
a kind of second nature to us. Later when this
strain of constant affection and indulgence slackened
off, as it normally does, we would tend to think we
were missing something essential.

(5) But the greatest cause of sadness is the
horror of suffering, a refusal of physical or moral
pain, seeing nothing but evil in it, not attending to
the good it brings with it, looking upon the slightest
difficulty as a tragedy and, with all this, an excessive
anticipation of future sufferings, imminent failure,
or a painful death.

Instead we should recall that events never turn out
so badly as we fear or so well as we dream they will.
There are many mistakes in our calculations about

the future. At the end of our life we shall discover
that we suffered by anticipation many ills which
never came our way at all. "Sufficient for the day is
the evil thereof," said Our Lord Jesus Christ. There
is no need to outdo Divine Providence. We know
that God will not permit greater sufferings than we
are able to bear, nor more sufferings than will be
useful to us. We also know that He Himself will
help us overcome them.

As for the thought of a painful death which pre-
disposes so many people to sadness, recall what doctors and actual experience teach us. Death will come
either from a paralysis of the brain, and then there is
no suffering because sensation is annihilated, or from
a paralysis of the heart or lungs, and then there
follows a state of stupefaction from the accumulation
of carbonic acid. In such a state there is no real
physical pain even though the body exhibits reflex
actions and contortions. As for moral suffering, the
Divine Goodness will take this away from those who
serve God with good will.

The immediate cause of the emotion of sadness
will always be, as we have indicated above, a thought
or idea of failure, frustration, lack, loss, or present
evil. Such a thought may exist clearly in our mind
or confusedly in our subconscious.

First Remedy

The first remedy is to take the ideas which cause
sadness in us and make them concrete, analyze them,
correct and control them. These may be ideas of
(a) failure or mistake, (b) inability or sickness,
(c) death of a loved one, (d) sorrow or trouble in
general.

(a) *Failure* in a career or business enterprise, or even being called upon to speak in public when unprepared, produces sadness when we think, "I have wasted my time, looked like a fool, or lost my head." In such instances happiness depends upon whether we are able to oppose this thought with a balancing truth such as, "I lost a dollar, but gained a million." This will always be a consoling truth if we act with a good intention. Whenever we are friends of God through grace and act with good will, our Heavenly Father writes for us a heavenly check for eternal glory and satisfaction. We have then gained a million, though we may have lost certain creatures, things of little value, insignificant grains of sand compared with the Infinite. Can such a situation be a sad one?

A mistake can be purely subjective when, for instance, we expect more than what is reasonable. But there is a means of ensuring joy. When we do favors for others, we should not look for human gratitude. For a human return is very often lacking, especially as regards work done for the common good. Let us act, instead, in order to please God who receives as done for Him what we do for our neighbor and who promises to pay us back with an "eternal kingdom."

(b) *Inability and sickness* sadden us with the idea that we are burdensome to others, do not produce anything, and merely suffer. The aged and infirm feel more strongly about this to the extent that their youth was active. If only they could understand that, for eternal results, patience and prayer are more effective than all our merely human initiative and activity.

I explained this to some old people in a nursing home and asked them to be missionaries through patience. Afterwards the nursing sisters could not get over their astonishment at seeing the vitality which this thought brought them. The same thing happened with a 12-year-old boy who had been in the hospital for three months. I asked him if he would like to be a missionary and save souls.

"But, Father, I can't even sit up in bed. I can hardly move."

"Exactly. If you offer your sufferings for souls, you can save them better than I. You see, Jesus Christ preached and performed many miracles, but only a few people were converted. When He suffered and died, though, He redeemed the whole world."

Hearing this, the youngster began to cry.

"Why are you crying?"

"Because I have lost a year of suffering. Why didn't someone tell me this a year ago?"

From then on he cried no more. Instead, the more he suffered, the happier he became. For he was helping to save more souls.

(c) *Death itself* cannot take joy away from a Christian family. If the death of a loved one makes us sad, this is usually because we look at him and imagine, like the pagans, that at death he has lost everything. Or because we look at ourselves and think that "we have lost him." This phrase is so often used erroneously. But if we activate our faith and convince ourselves of the happiness of those who die in the Lord, and the help which, with Him, they can bring us, then we can feel consolation and joy.

(d) *A present difficulty or "trouble"* will not make

us sad if, instead of looking at its unpleasant side, we see it in the light of faith. Suffering should be an imitation of God who took suffering upon Himself in this life. Our pain is a completion of what is lacking, as St. Paul says, in the sufferings of Christ. It makes the application of the merits of His Passion more effective. More souls can be saved as a result of our sufferings if they are united with those of Christ.

Trouble is a check drawn upon the bank of heaven. If we understand God's own language, we would read in it this idea: "Infinite Justice and Goodness promise to pay back in heaven a superhuman and endless glory and satisfaction to the Christian who, while in the state of grace, willingly accepts a light and passing suffering." The divine signature is put on this check only when we accept the suffering. Day by day to pile up such checks for eternity is a source of happiness; and it is a great good fortune to suffer only lightly and for an instant as the price of gaining infinite joy forever.

We must know how to value suffering and how to handle the thorns of life. If we tread on them, they torment us; in our conscience they kill us; in our heart they stir up life. Under our feet they prevent our walking; in our conscience they block true life; in our heart they let us fly. This power they have from the Heart of Christ.

Second Remedy

The second remedy is to *foment thoughts of joy*. We should always have optimistic thoughts, happy memories, and a clear acknowledgement of God's benefits in that treasure house of creation, human nature. We should also increase our knowledge and cheerfully think about the inexhaustible treasures offered us in the world of color, form, and sound. Artists usually catch a vision of all this and know how to appreciate it.

Our eyes are marvelously perfect cameras. Automatically they focus upon, capture, and project into our brain living scenes in full color and three dimensions. Our sense of hearing is like a marvelous internal musical instrument which faithfully reproduces thousands of different notes and melodies. Our hands, arms and legs are like cranes which can execute an infinite variety of complicated movements. In brief, our whole organism is a marvelous treasure created for us by God. This is especially true of our memory, a library which classifies, in order, thousands of useful experiences; our understanding which continually discovers more and more of reality and will be able to understand Infinite Reality; and our will by which we are capable of union with Uncreated Goodness.

Recognize, too, the many goods we have in the family, State, and Church, and all the supernatural means we have of getting to Heaven. This is a happy thought because of the certitude we have from faith and reason that God exists and is Our Father, that He is with us, watches over us, and governs all our circumstances for our benefit. This is, moreover, a calming and peaceful thought, for hope in the divine promises gives us a foretaste of Heaven. There is, in addition, a thrill of joy and satisfaction in the thought that we are the objects of God's love and can ourselves sincerely love Him.

Third Remedy

The third remedy is to *change* negative attitudes and habits, which are the cause of sadness and depression, for those which are positive and joyful. We should get used to extracting from ordinary day-to-day life whatever can increase our joy, rest, and legitimate satisfaction, and whatever can fill us with optimism. We should avoid the thoughts which bring disillusionment, envy, or discouragement. To this end we should act as follows.

(a) *Lead a simpler life,* with fewer demands for food, rest, entertainment, travel, and so on. Learn how to find satisfaction in a modest quantity of all these things. There you have the secret of happiness and equanimity. Many millionaires are pressured by worries, ulcers and insomnia. They yearn longingly for the days of their youth. They may have worked very hard when they were young, but at that time an ordinary meal gave them full satisfaction, a hard bed perfect repose, and a simple game in the open fields complete diversion.

(b) *Find enjoyment in your work.* If you do not, a negative emotion of impatience or disgust will constantly be nagging at you. We should find pleasure in a job well done, useful for others, and of value to ourselves in eternity. Then there will be no time to be bored. An idle life that needs continual and costly entertainment may satisfy a child, but no adult can find completion in it. For an adult needs to be convinced that he is using his time to some avail.

(c) Make your life one of *continual satisfaction and positive feelings.* Obviously there will be inter-

ruptions in this satisfaction when we run into evident
negligence, incompetence, or bad will. But even
these will have excusing or attenuating causes. And
if we look at what patience can produce for us in
Heaven, these occasions may even bring us joy. Let
us not bemoan the inevitable, bad weather, etc.
Neither should we attempt what is impossible. On
the contrary, look for and find in your existential
situations motives of joy and satisfaction: the blue
of the skies, colors of the field, the habits of birds
and insects, the variety and beauty of flowers, plants,
and sounds. In the roof which protects us, the hearts
which love us, society that helps us, God Himself
is caring for us and preparing us with an Infinite
Love for a happiness to come which is more than
human. So look for the good in all things and find
pleasure in cooperating with it. Always have a
pleasant and kind word to say that will bring joy
to others, cheer to yourself, and peace all round. A
"Thank you" to the porter, elevator operator, or taxi
driver costs nothing, but can sweeten an embittered
life.

One man in Havana came to me to seek a remedy
for his "great unhappiness." He had a wife with a
defect which made her hard to live with. This defect
was a temperamental one, and she was hardly
responsible for it at all. I asked him to come back
again in two days and, in the meanwhile, to think
over and write down his wife's good qualities. He
came back to thank me, already cured. He understood that he had a precious diamond with 33
brilliant sides to it and only one small scratch on its
surface.

Fourth Remedy

The fourth remedy is the expression of joy, a *smile*, even when our negative thoughts and attitudes have lasted so long that they have engraved in us a feeling or tendency to sadness. We must try to implant the contrary feeling even in the subconscious. Do that by joyful thoughts and conversation and, most of all, by that expression of satisfaction, a smile. This satisfaction and joy should be expressed with one's whole being, an open laugh, smiling eyes, cheerful words, a happy song, a contented tone of voice, relaxed breathing. We should smile *joyfully* when things go well, and *bravely* in time of suffering.

(a) Smile *when things go well* and everything is on your side, when you can seize upon the great good that there is in the world, the good you possess yourself and that others have, and all the good that God wishes to give you. This external expression of satisfaction helps to tone up the whole organism, facilitates the process of nutrition, and relaxes tension. With joy our understanding is sharper, our thinking clearer, our imagination more vivid, our soul more serene, and our will stronger. A pleasant smile attracts one's neighbor, glorifies God, makes virtue easy and sacrifice sweet.

(b) You should also smile *bravely in sorrow*. Whenever you suffer, deliberately have more joy, like the organist who overcomes outside noise by playing the organ with vigor. Smile to convince yourself that the little misfortunes and indispositions that would tend to make a strong impression on you are really insignificant. By smiling accelerate a positive reaction against the very first movements of impatience or disgust. Smile at once to block the very first depressing tendency or its growth. Smile and sing to get the strength to act "as if" you were content. There is no way to prevent you from being happy at all times because the one thing necessary, doing God's will, is always near at hand.

In Brazil I was asked to visit a lady who had spent six months without going out of her house, always weeping and wailing over the death of her son. Her sleep and appetite were gone. She seemed to be on the brink of moral and physical breakdown, despite the medications prescribed by her doctor. As soon as I arrived, she cried out, "I am so unhappy. Six months ago I lost my son." Because she was a Christian and because her son had died as a good Christian, I said to her, "Lady, take that back! Six months ago you gained your son." And I explained this to her graphically to make an impression on her imagination. "You were going along in one ship across the stormy sea of life, and your son in another. All of a sudden a friendly wind and a friendly hand brought your son to the safe harbor of salvation while you go on, tossed about by the storms of life. Isn't it true that six months ago you gained your son?" She accepted the explanation, but with her intellect only. To complete her cure, feelings had to enter. So I then said, "Say after me, and in the same tone of voice as I, this sentence: I am happy, for six months ago I gained my son." It cost her a great deal to repeat that sentence and to produce the tone of satisfaction with which I pronounced it. But when she understood my explanation, that this very tone of voice would produce in her the feeling of joy that she needed, she repeated it so earnestly that she was immediately transformed.

EXISTENTIAL SADNESS AND ANXIETY

Sometimes sadness and fear can have roots that are very deep and far reaching. A vague idea of loss or danger can seem to be part of one's very being and dominate everything earthly and passing. This often happens in people without sufficient faith or religious practice. Their innate tendency toward God and toward true and endless happiness seems to have been repressed and frustrated. This can cause painful feelings and even bring them to a neurotic state. According to Dr. Viktor Frankl, one-third of the neuroses in Europe have this as their cause. The remedy consists in allowing our transcendental tendencies to extend themselves outward by means of a more perfectly realized knowledge of a personal God, who is our Father, governing the universe for our good and by a more perfect realization of the end for which we have been placed in this world—that is, to love and serve this Heavenly Father and afterwards enjoy His company forever in heaven.

We ought to put aside at once, then, every sad thought or memory and think habitually about the treasures we do possess, natural or supernatural, present or future. Keep the following sayings in mind, after meditating upon them, and they will help you accomplish this.

All goes well, for everywhere God stands as a loving Father behind everything and guiding every event beforehand.

I cannot be sad, granted that the Infinite God loves me and wants me to be happy.

Suffering is a check drawn upon heaven which brings joy to the noblest part of my being.

We are worth what we can redeem; the size of our cross is the measure of our greatness.

My life will be very useful; by prayer and suffering I can save many souls.

Be happy because at every moment you can be as pleasing to God as possible by doing what He wants and wanting what He does.

My happiness is immense, for a God of love dwells in my soul through grace.

The best remedy for sadness is to learn how to be happy. This is explained in the following chapter where we gather together in one place those ideas that are scattered through the whole book.

remember, you can keep "suffering" the natural resistance to the Cross, but not "surrender" to it by trying to "convince" your mind with the Truths of Faith. The Hidden life which the natural mind can't see. the life with this "personal God" - Nature won't disapear, but the Hidden life of the soul will get over it, upon it, above the Nature step by step

XIV

How to Be Happy

HAPPINESS IS NOT found, but made. It does not depend on what you do not have, but on the use you make of what you do have. It is not something far from yourself but the most intimate part of your being. It is the consciousness of a good, and the greater and more lasting this is, the greater will be your happiness.

You need not travel many lands to find happiness, nor burden yourself with back-breaking labors to win it. It is enough to follow your own road, the road of duty. If you can control your thoughts, you will be able to find the flower of joy even among the thorns of suffering.

We all strive for happiness. God wants us to be happy. He repeats it a thousand times in the Scripture and liturgy. "My peace I leave with you." "Your joy no one will take from you." "Rejoice always in the Lord." "Alleluia." Joy is possible, then, in all circumstances of life.

However, there are many who do not find it because they go looking for it where it is not to be found, in vice or illicit pleasure. And so, upon returning within themselves, they find their heart empty and feel tedium, disgust and sadness. They try to forget by means of amusements, movies, parties, novels, and so on. But they do not get rid of the cause of their unhappiness, nor do they give their heart the satisfaction of duty done. They are satisfied with merely hiding their lack of happiness.

"Joy," says Aristotle, "is the accompaniment of a perfect act." Now an act against conscience or duty is essentially vitiated or imperfect. It can then produce, even after some momentary delight, only a deep and lasting sadness. But even those who strive for joy where it may be found sometimes find only suffering, and because of this they drown themselves in a sea of sadness. Yet suffering should not be an obstacle to your joy. The bee draws honey from flowers, and the soul can draw honey from thorns. But this process is patented—in Christianity.

OBJECTIVE SUFFERING

Suffering can be an objective thing; for example, the sickness, poverty or failures which God positively wants you to suffer. It can also be mostly subjective, the effects which the first type produces in you and which you do not control. These effects are sadness, worry and fear which God only permits. Here what He positively wants is your reaction to them, your control of them.

Be happy, then, "negatively" by overcoming objective suffering. Convert it into joy. How? By shifting your gaze from the unpleasant aspect, from the ugly face of suffering, and concentrating on the bright side. Mentally you have this power, acquired by the re-education of concentration. (See Part I.)

Suffering actually has two sides to it, a pleasant

and unpleasant side. The unpleasant side contradicts your tendencies, sensuality, natural inclinations, pride, self-will. Do not fix your attention on this unpleasant side. Suffering has a pleasant side also. In the natural order suffering can be pleasant because it brings an increase of experience, strength, counsel, and patience. But this natural side alone is but small consolation. Hence the difficulty in comforting atheists, but how easy to comfort Christians! Considered in the supernatural order, suffering is exceedingly attractive. It is the role which, while on earth, God chose for Himself. It is the livery of Jesus Christ. It is a check which God offers us. If we accept it, God signs it and our happiness in Heaven will be proportionate to its value. It is the secret treasure of the Cross, made known to and through the saints. And it is the fruit of devotion to the Heart of Jesus. Supernaturally, then, we are able to increase this inclination to suffering and find our joy in it. It is integral to Christianity, the apex of virtue, the grandeur of the saints whose joy no human event could disturb.

St. Paul said, "I am filled with joy because of my tribulations." St. Peter recommended, "Be filled with joy in your sufferings." The Apostles "left the tribunal joyfully because they had been judged worthy to suffer insults and sorrow for Jesus Christ."

St. Ignatius Loyola attained complete dominion over his feelings. The doctor forbade him to think about sad things. He examined himself. The saddest of all would be the total destruction of the Society of Jesus. Yet he decided that fifteen minutes of prayer would be enough to reconcile himself even to this.

St. Francis Xavier had such consolation in the Molucca Islands where he suffered so much that he exclaimed, "It is enough, Lord. I shall die of joy."

St. Theresa used to repeat, "Either to suffer or to die." And St. Mary Magdalene de Pazzi used to say, "Not to die, but to suffer!"

On the missions, as a matter of fact, the missionary's greatest consolation after a day of suffering is to repeat before the Tabernacle, "For you, O Lord!"

It is within your power, then, to change objective suffering into joy instead of sorrow.

SUBJECTIVE SORROW

In the face of present or imminent disgrace any normal person first feels a sense of dejection and worry. But by considering its attractive aspect he soon controls these feelings and they do not last very long. However, in sick or nervous people such feelings keep coming back and become obsessions. They produce persistent sadness, phobias, or scruples which destroy all peace and joy. These are crosses which God permits, but which He wants you to control. You must then fight and get control of them.

Control of Subjective Sorrow

1. In addition to the explanations in Chapter X, in case of sorrow or internal conflict, *express your feelings externally* in consultation. Make them known as soon as possible to your director or confessor. Tell him of moral acts which burden your conscience, harrowing doubts or indecisions, fears which get control of you. This manifestation with its psychological and supernatural solution will resolve your internal conflict and sorrow.

2. *Live in the present.* The present is a fount of joy. There are delights which crave to be yours. They are external creation (esthetic pleasure) and moral beauty. So give them entrance by attending to the present. You should not think about the sorry past which has already slipped from your hands. Leave it to the mercy of God. And think not on the agony of an uncertain future. Leave this to His providence. The present is a pleasant path which runs between two chasms, the past and the future. Whoever by sadness or scruples falls into the past, or slips by worry into the future, ceases advancing toward his happiness.

Latin theme for the worriers Romans.

3. *Live a conscious life.* "*Age quod agis*" ("Do what you're doing"). If you work on a conscious level, fear, worry and sadness will find no place to torment you. Thus you will lessen and even suppress the influence of a sad and uncontrolled subconscious. "We stand in need of happy people," writes Marden, "who look away from the sinful, bitter and perverse world and turn toward God's world to admire its beauty and perfection."

4. *Practice voluntary concentration on other matters.* These concentrations may be indifferent in relation to those which the unconscious tries to impose on you. If sadness or worry is besieging you, concentrate on some study or occupation that pleases you. Even better, concentrate on something directly opposed. For instance, against fear or disturbance concentrate on living images of peace, control and energy. In this war you must take the offensive in order to rout the enemy even from his lair in the unconscious.

Cultivate the habit of joy. Your mental make-up is a labyrinthine wood. Your thoughts and acts are men who are tracing a path through it. Where one has passed, the easier it is for the next. So then, if you would win the heights of joy, you must send joyful thoughts through to open up the trail. Repeat them and reinforce them with acts of satisfaction and optimism until you have enlarged the trail and made it firm through habit. Then, almost without noticing it, you will find you are always happy.

5. *Practice will acts.* Will the contrary feeling; that is, be animated, tranquil, kind, happy. Talk and work *as if* you did not feel the opposite feeling (antipathy, worry, fear) or *as if* you were animated, happy, and so forth. (saying to yourself : I want this, I want to do that) —etc

6. *Use suggestion.* At night before falling beneath the dominion of the unconscious and in the morning when leaving its control, think with feeling about images of peace, control and joy. Repeat to yourself: "Everything I do can be a step taken nearer to God," "Every day I am increasing in sanctifying grace," "Every day I am happier."

7. *Moderate your desires and aspirations.* Keep them within reasonable limits. Seek not for body or soul or anything else a greater security, health or prosperity than God wishes it to have in this world. Thus scruples or worry will lessen or disappear.

8. *Overcome negative and depressing feelings.* Do this by introducing other feelings which are positive, sublime and ennobling, such as love of an ideal, of God, souls, or Heaven. Overcome petty, low and disordered self-love with true love of your-

self and your spiritual and eternal good. Before this sublime reality all fears, sadness and phobias fall to earth.

Happiness in this life is not divorced from sacrifice. Our satisfaction increases in the measure that we make those who surround us happy, that we seek the greater glory of God, and in proportion to what we sacrifice to this end.

POSITIVE HAPPINESS

You can have a happiness and joy which is not external and vain but interior, true and well-founded, one which fills your heart with satisfaction. This happiness has four aspects and comes to us through as many channels:

Aesthetic pleasure by which we receive within us the beauty of the external world through conscious sensations, when we contemplate the beauties of nature or of the arts, and especially when we do this in the light and warmth of an ideal. (Cf. Chapters III, VII, XV.)

Intellectual pleasure when by intellectual concentration we possess the truth with certitude, and perfect it or complete it by analysis and synthesis. (Cf. Chapter III.)

Volitional satisfaction in the power of producing, and in doing, what we value. This type of happiness is the result of exercising a firm and constant will (Chapters III and VII); and finally,—

Emotional or affective satisfaction at feeling one's own kindness irradiating others, and the kindness of others being diffused in oneself through the elevation and equanimity of our feelings (Chapters V, X, XIV).

Your human capital is twofold: your faculties and the time for making them produce. You can have no true satisfaction if you see your capital diminishing each day, yet bring you no return. Nor can you have any satisfaction if you feel your time passing in useless amusements or occupations. You ought not to feel that each passing moment is lost or less profitable. You should feel that it is a source of your own and your neighbor's well-being, and a fruitful seed of an immortal and happy life in Heaven.

To bring about this satisfaction and sense of fulfillment, the "life" element should also be present in a vigorous functioning of your intellect and will. Then you will find in your mental concept of happiness the characteristics of unity and totality.

The scholar who makes a discovery has great intellectual pleasure. The mother who is always loving and showing her love for her child is very happy even in the midst of work and sufferings. If that pleasure of the scholar were not disturbed by other ideas and distractions and were prolonged by new and more brilliant findings, and if that of the mother had as its object not a mortal child with all its imperfections but one which would never be separated from her and had all possible good qualities, then we would have true, complete mental happiness. Before it, all merely bodily happiness would grow pale, fade and pass away. You could sum it up in these words: *fullness and unity of your mind and feelings*.

Now let us see how this happiness, though limited in this world, yet unlimited, secure and eternal in the next, is in a real and true sense near at hand.

With re-education of control presupposed, apply your understanding to knowing not some small part of the truth but all the truth, infinite truth, truth in itself, God. Each day you can discover new horizons without ever exhausting this infinite fountain of truth and beauty. This is the joy of spiritual persons at receiving in prayer those supernatural lights which we call divine consolations. These eclipse all worldly happiness and cannot even be imagined by those who have not experienced them.

Dedicate your will and feelings to loving the infinitely lovable good, God. Strive to realize that He is not far off from you, but close by in all created things. In these He is at your service and gives you joy. Try to possess Him in the Eucharist, human in body as you yourself. And enjoy a holy intimacy with Him, present as He is within you through sanctifying grace.

This is the type of joy in union with God that made a St. Francis of Assisi complain of the sun that it rose too early and forced him to leave the delights of a night with God. Happiness impelled St. Ignatius, when he saw a flower, to say with tears of consolation, "Be silent, be quiet for I understand you." He would remain in ecstatic contemplation of the Divine Beauty of which the flower was but a pale reflection.

Speaking before a Youth Congress of Catholic Action, one of the leaders said, "At first in prayer I used to look toward Heaven, but ever since I realized that God was within me, I look toward myself and feel great joy." Tears came to his eyes and were joined to those of his listeners. He was happy at loving and feeling God within himself. That is why

the great mystics who felt the presence of God in this world speak so many marvels about this little-known happiness.

St. John of the Cross insists that the devil admitted to him that if he had a body and if, in order to see God, he would have to climb a pole studded with thorns and needles, he would not hesitate to do this for ten thousand years in exchange for enjoying the sight of God for a single minute.

Some Thoughts on Changing Sorrow into Joy

Passing over the threshing floor, the southwest wind raises eddies of dust. But, sweeping through flower gardens, it raises a cloud of perfumes. So does the wind of suffering act differently in different souls.

The Divine Heart of infinite happiness is "bound with thorns." If you feel the touch of thorns in your heart, it is a sign that God is reaching out His heart to you, a sign of the embrace of Infinite Happiness. But happiness will enter into you only through your wounds. God left a trail of blood at His passage through the world; no longer can there be doubt about which is the path to glory, the road to permanent happiness.

Acceptance of sorrow is a contract for work made with God. You agree to construct some great thing with Him. You are the workman who does not see the plans. God is the architect with sublime and magnificent designs.

Nothing great is accomplished without suffering and humiliation, says Newman, and everything is possible by using these means. We must be friendly with suffering. It is a selfless and faithful friend who

reminds us of true goods. Souls are instructed by word of mouth but are saved by sacrifice.

Some Thoughts on Happiness and Joy

Happiness is a noble, peaceful and recollected lady who dwells in the hidden fortress of the soul. She knows and tastes its treasures. Frequently she shows herself at the windows of the face and wreathes it with a smile. She clothes the face thus with the brilliance of rational being. This is something about which neither animals nor the most beautiful flowers can boast.

When the polished, peaceful mirror of consciousness reflects a ray of the sun, some good possessed or soon to come, its spontaneous reflection is joy, a smile. If the sun of Infinite Good shines directly upon it, it will reflect happiness.

Life should be a perpetual joy, the joy of living for God, of serving Him in one's neighbor, of saving souls, the austere joy found in suffering. There is the joy of living in a present of infinite value, joy for a past entrusted to the Divine Mercy, joy for a future assured by His Paternal Providence. Have joy in work, and if this is beyond your powers, then have joy in prayer. If even this seems impossible for you, then have joy at least in suffering in Christ and for the sake of Heaven.

The apostle who takes doctrine and example and, together with these, sows smiles, and then waters these with prayers and sacrifices, will win many souls. "Joy," says St. Paul of the Cross, "is the sun of souls. It enlightens those who possess it and enlivens as many as receive its rays."

The exercise of Christian charity is the best way

to make yourself joyful. And this is your most effective contribution to the happiness of others. Smiling eyes scatter more rays of joy than precious diamonds. Through joy you will better perform your duties. And your burdens will be lighter. It will be your consolation in solitude and your best introduction to society. You will be the more sought after, the more trusted and better appreciated.

The vicious, degenerate or low person may come on the stage of life as a loud and vulgar jester. But he is almost never sincerely happy. Almost never can he wholly forget what weighs upon his conscience. Evil is a cold hand which freezes smiles. But a frank and hearty smile is almost always an indication of a noble and pure heart. The virtue that smiles is the more beautiful and often the most heroic.

OUTLINE DIAGRAM

❦

How to Be Happy

N E G A T I V E L Y

God wants you to be happy
- not in vice, nor only in amusements
- but in duty, and within you.

Objective suffering
(accept the disgraces, etc. which God wants you to)
- Avoid pessimism
  - contrary to desires, feelings, instincts
- Cultivate optimism
  - natural
    - gives experience, strength, counsel
  - supernatural
    - Cross of Christ
    - His role on earth
    - a check drawn on Heaven
    - the great Architect
    - example of the Saints

Subjective sorrow
(which depends on you)
- by expression, confidence, confession
- live in the present (aesthetic pleasure)
- conscious life
- concentration on joyful things
- contrary actions and will acts
- suggestion of peace and joy
- moderated desires
- deep emplanting of sublime feelings

P O S I T I V E L Y

Intellectual
- a scholar's pleasure at attaining some truth
- unlimited joy with all truth

Affective
- a mother's happiness in loving her child
- highest happiness in loving and possessing all Goodness

Examples and sayings

XV

Choice of a Vision for One's Life

*A great life is the great dream of youth
realized in mature age.*   Alfred de Vigny

ALL THE ADVICE OF THIS BOOK can be summarized
into the choosing of an ideal vision for one's
life. This is a short-cut to attain what we propose
in the second part of the book. It is medicine,
strength, joy, activity, and rest. It has produced
geniuses, heroes, and saints.

There is a general or abstract ideal (learning, for
example, or art, skill, service, sanctity, patriotism)
which can be the goal of your actions. And this goal
you can strip in your own mind of all possible defects
and adorn with all good qualities. This becomes your
particular ideal. The ideal chosen by you becomes
the object of a tendency or inclination. It is a
detailed picture of your forceful and permanent
desire of the more general goal.

THE NATURE OF AN IDEAL

The Intellectual Element

There is especially required, as the very word
"ideal" indicates, a great idea (the general ideal).

[241]

This is a concrete and constant idea, a goal, a purpose, a good that is precisely, clearly and constantly foreseen. It is a fixed idea, a permanent attention, with all the power of concentration and action which this implies: "Fear the man of a single idea," says an old proverb.

The Feeling Element

Your ideal results in a fixed and instinctive tendency, at the same time sensible and spiritual. You are in a state of forceful impulse toward that good which constantly presents itself as fulfilling the aspirations of your being. It tends to attract related inclinations to itself and its own direction, and to repel opposed ones.

The Will or Executive Element

That permanent attention and feeling influences your will. As a result your will acquires a new force and constancy. And your ideal is then translated into repeated acts. It is axiomatic that a fixed idea and constant tendency impel to action.

FALSE IDEAL OR EVIL PASSION

This, too, will constantly influence your will, hence its great strength. But it is the desire of an evil which is, by supposition, presented as a good (that is, disordered sexual passion, passion for gambling, intoxication, undue ambition). It does have some good as its object (pleasure, the momentary physical good of some tendency or of one of the senses). And this fixed idea is associated with remembered feelings of pleasure already experienced. It fills the field of consciousness and leaves no room for reflec-

tion upon the fact that this momentary partial good of merely one part of your being sometimes leads to sickness, to a lasting general damage of the body. Or the pleasure is forbidden because such a false ideal involves moral evil, disease of the soul, sin. It may eventually bring on the physical, final total evil of both soul and body in an eternity of shame.

Evil passion disunites, unbalances you by making you seek a partial good which is incapable of satisfying your instinctive tendency toward your whole good. Hence it will cause you an intimate sense of sorrow, feelings of sadness, restlessness, lack of mental control. Your personality will not be secure, but will find itself wandering astray from the path.

TRUE IDEALS

Effects of a True Ideal

A noble ideal gives unity, harmony, vigor and fullness to life and increases the physical and mental perfection of your acts. Unity of thought and desire does away with parasite ideas, makes concentration easy, brings pleasure and maximum return to work and study.

A Latin student used to hate this subject and failed it three times. But the ideal of literature and oratory still shone brightly in his mind. So it was easy to make him understand how useful and necessary Latin is to this end. At last the hated subject was overlaid with joyful colors and in his next examination he received a very high rating.

Singleness of thought, as we said in Part One, is not fatiguing. And because it is pleasant, it is conducive to rest. And so the ideal which makes you think steadily of what you most desire is a source of

rest and joy. This is the reason, in cases of "over-work," for the effort to discover the patient's interests or ideals in order to help him to rest.

Many energies for your education and perfection are released by the ideal. The ideal of patriotism has made heroes of many timid souls. That of scholarship or research has fostered much constancy and pleasure in overcoming difficulties. The ideal of sanctity, or the priesthood, or that of the Christian family has preserved countless youths unspotted among the sloughs of sensuality.

The ideal of consoling Jesus Christ in His weak or sickly members has aroused and sustained holocausts of self-sacrifice and charity in asylums and hospitals. And the ideal of winning new cities and nations to Him has appealed to adventurous souls ever since the first Pentecost. Saul of Tarsus and Francis Xavier are each a colossus of heroism and superhuman grandeur, the fruits of this ideal. And they lead along behind them thousands of self-sacrificing and valiant missionaries. One aspirant to the apostolate among pagans used to say, "The ideal of my whole life is to sacrifice everything, furrow the seas, suffer everything, save one soul, then die."

As the ideal issues in a permanently vitalizing tendency, it attracts other unopposed inclinations to itself. The contrary ones it annihilates or weakens by leaving no room in the mind for the type of thought or feeling they feed upon. Your happiness increases because of this unity and exuberance of your intellectual and emotional life. You experience the natural joy of perfect acts and the profound satisfaction which follows upon merit and moral goodness.

Ignatius of Loyola fell wounded in the battle of Pamplona. His human, knightly ideal was turned into a divine ideal on contact with the *Lives of the Saints* and the *Life of Christ*. His ideal became "The greater glory of the great King." And his life was transformed into one of marvelous efficiency, unshakable peace and superhuman heroism.

HOW TO CHOOSE YOUR IDEAL

1. Choose an ideal which will not be in conflict with your total good (that is, with your final goal in life), but which will further it and make it easier to attain. Your main purpose in this life is to prepare for the next.

Caesar, Alexander the Great, and Napoleon each had an ideal of conquest which gave unity and efficiency to their lives. But the good they sought was a partial one and did not satisfy the whole soul. Moreover, it brought evil upon many peoples and nations, and was barren of happiness. All three have left us their admissions of disillusionment.

Cicero and Demosthenes had the ideal of rising in eloquence to direct their country and correct abuses. This good was ever before their eyes, ever the object of their desire. It made them overcome difficulties, attain great success, and enjoy profound satisfaction. But lower objectives filtered into their ideal, and so it did not fulfill the aspirations of their whole being.

2. Choose an ideal in agreement with your aptitudes and personality.

The Spanish historian, Menéndez Pelayo, considered the black legend spread throughout historical

writing about Spanish Catholicism in its "Golden Age." He conceived the ideal of defending his country and religion from such great calumnies. So he studied and surpassed his colleagues in learning and elegance of style. His books astonished the world and he lived an intensely happy life while writing his marvelous *Historia de los Heterodoxas Españoles*. He lived a full life and had a happy death.

3. Let your ideal be found outside of and superior to yourself. Otherwise, you could say with a famous novelist, "Charlie is a little state bounded on the north, east, south and west by Charlie." If your ideal is your body, its boundaries are limited indeed. Corruption and death come after but a few years.

The ideal of life is the development of the whole being for the profit of others and the service of God. It is the transfiguration of our instincts into a higher spiritual love. It is living in oneself and not, as it were, apart from oneself; among others and not apart from them; in God and not apart from Him (José Serre).

4. Let your ideal be practical and bring you to act at the present moment on the good thought or noble purpose you have. Do not forget that, as Lemoine puts it, "the most beautiful moment in life, the richest and most significant for the future is the present moment; at the present moment you can amend the past and construct the future." And in the present minute you can glorify the Infinite Being and by saving souls set new jewels in the divine crown of His external glory. You may say that an ideal is not perfect which cannot be realized at every instant.

"If I cannot now realize my ideal," says Adela Kann, "at least I want to idealize my reality."

The greatest ideal of life is to realize at every instant the ideal of God, His most holy will. Or put it this way: to feel yourself in all things in harmony with the thought of your Creator. "The ideal of life is to live it fully and with delight," we may say with Jeglot. The ideal is to have a healthful care of one's physical life, an unlimping moral life (duty, justice, truth), a serious and orderly intellectual life, a life of the heart with a twofold movement (giving oneself and guarding oneself). The ideal is, above all, an intense spiritual life which is at the present moment clear, deep and primarily interior. Then it will later be an apostolic one. And the ideal life should also be joyful, for service, prayer and even suffering should enter into the great joy which is God.

5. Your ideal should be concrete and summed up in a few words to be frequently repeated.

John Berchmans understood the heroism of duty perfectly done even in the smallest affairs. "*Maximus in minimis*," he would say to himself. "I shall be outstanding in the smallest things." And he reached sanctity at the age of twenty-two. Stanislaus Kostka, hero and saint at eighteen years, made it concrete for himself thus: "I was not born for present things but for the future, for higher things *(ad altiora natus sum)*."

THE IDEAL OF IDEALS

If the infinitely perfect God were to become incarnate, this God-Man would then be the ideal of humanity.

Now it is a fact that the supreme Grandeur, unlimited Goodness, eternal Truth, infinite Beauty, God, was not only made man, our equal, companion and model, but also willed to be the price of our ransom on the Cross, the food of our souls in the Eucharist and our reward in Heaven.

This God-Man, with all the rights of Creator and Redeemer, of excellence, wisdom and goodness, who wishes to reign over men and who alone offers them their greatest good in time and eternity, is not only not loved and obeyed by them all, but very many are ignorant of Him, forget and insult Him. And not a few of those who say they are His offend Him or give Him only fragments of their heart, the scraps of their love.

Yet instead of hurling sentence of condemnation He opens His breast, shows you His wounded Heart. With cries of love He says to you, "You, at least, love and console Me, make Me reign." He offers you the consoling pact He made with St. Margaret Mary: "Take care of Me and My affairs, and I shall care for you and yours." He will provide for your temporal and eternal good, your health, life, family, business, your soul, its virtues and eternal salvation. He will do this in the measure in which you give Him pleasure and glory. When you ratify this pact, all worries, scruples and phobias disappear. Your supreme good is to be taken care of by Another who understands it better than you do yourself. He wills it Himself and can procure it for you.

Elements of This Ideal

1. Surrender the past to His mercy and the future to His providence in order to live a happy life in

the present. Surrender body and soul and everything to Him, for Him to care and provide for according to His will.

2. Take as your one and only ideal for every instant the giving to Him of the greatest possible pleasure by duty done, charity for your neighbor, the apostolate of souls and fervent prayer. Summarize it thus: "Most loving King, loved and insulted, I wish always to do everything the better to love, console and glorify You."

3. When your heart is freed from other affections, worries and desires, give entire possession of it to "the Heart which loves and is not loved." Enthrone Him in your heart. Make Him absolute and sovereign King of it to console Him for the sharp wound caused by chosen souls who do not receive Him or give Him only a corner of their hearts.

4. Feel His loving Presence in you by sanctifying grace, adore Him, give Him company in this living temple. Above all, consult His desires and ask His orders. Let Him reign in your senses, faculties, feelings and works.

Effects of This Ideal

There are wonderful promises made to those truly devoted to His Heart. They will have blessings on all their undertakings, peace, fervor, sanctity, eternal salvation, an effective apostolate.

1. Mentally you will obtain the change of sorrow into joy. You will see suffering as very attractive since the King, Infinite Wisdom, chose suffering for

Himself. Crowned with thorns, He Himself asks for victims to help Him by voluntary suffering to placate the justice of God and save souls.

2. You will obtain the unification of your life through this sublime ideal. It is an ideal which is realizable at each and every moment. You will overcome that bothersome duality of mental life, phobias, worries and subjective sorrow.

3. You will obtain a consoling fullness of your intellectual and emotional life by knowing, loving and possessing Infinite Truth and Goodness. This will happen in a most attractive and intimate manner, that is, by the God-Man dwelling within you, opening His breast to show you His Heart, impatient with love for you and struck by sorrow when you do not permit Him to give you even greater gifts.

Such a happy person as this, dominated by the interests and person of Him who takes possession of it and reigns completely in its depths, who communicates to it His own peace, happiness and life, is like the clear, crystal water of a quiet lake. Human events will, like gentle breezes, scarcely trouble the surface of the water and will not disturb the clear image of blue sky, symbol of divine peace and happiness, which are common to both hearts, the throne-heart and the Heart Enthroned.

OUTLINE DIAGRAM

❧◦❧

Choice of an Ideal Vision
for One's Life

False ideal { idea, tendency and will fixed upon evil
this causes turbulence and disunion

T
R
U
E

I
D
E
A
L

Effects { unifies and harmonizes life
gives concentration and efficiency
helps rest and enjoyment
perfects and dignifies

Choice of an ideal { in harmony with your ultimate end
conformed to your aptitudes
outside of and superior to yourself
practicable, realizable at every instant
make it concrete in a few words

Ideal of ideals, Christ the King

object { most noble: the ideal Man
most lovable: Love that is not loved
most useful: that He might reign in all men

concrete { contract, unconditional surrender
He will take care of you
"whatever pleases Him more"
motive: to love and console Him
method: make Him King of your heart and accompany H
obey Him, identify yourself with Him and His interes

effects

spiritual—His promises { peace, fervor
blessing, salvation
effective production

mental { unification of life
change of sorrow into joy
killing of phobias
consoling fullness of life of { intellect
feelings

XVI

Résumé

(Directives for Health and Efficiency)

1. Be conscious of your mental and bodily capital. Recognize the limitations of your strength. If this has been depleted by an extraordinary or prolonged effort, know how to replenish it in time by proportionate rest. Do not prolong concentration of attention for more than two hours without a few minutes of conscious sensations and muscular relaxation. The sick, weak and convalescent should abbreviate their effort all the more.

2. Do your job or everyday duty with the greatest possible perfection, that is, with concentration, naturalness and pleasure. Avoid all tension, haste and disgust. Find in your work the strength and joy of an ideal. *"Age quod agis,"* "Do what you're doing."

3. Do not try to realize at the instant *all* the good and greatness to which your impulses urge you, but only what is possible *at the time* and which a tranquil judgment shows you is proportioned to your abilities.

4. In time of relaxation avoid exaggerated competition. Recognize and accept the physical, intellectual and moral superiority of others. If you must be pre-eminent in something, let it be in goodness, understanding and patience.

5. In time of failure or adversity, know how to find and how to reflect on the goodness or usefulness this offers for yourself or others, for time or for eternity. Set this counterweight against excessive sadness and discouragement. Accept the inevitable and base your ideal upon it. This will be the secret of your efficiency and happiness.

6. Avoid the tension which comes from doubt and insecurity about your health, skill, and temporal or eternal success. Trust in your strength and divine aid. Let religious faith and tranquility of conscience be your guarantee.

7. Make use of the greatest of your faculties by means of deliberate, concrete and motivated decisions. Then put them into execution without fatigue or further discussion. This will give you a strong and healthy personality.

8. Recognize the double tendency in you: the angel and the beast. Make the higher level of life control and rule the lower levels. Make the good of your whole being keep its supremacy over sense pleasure, caprice or the good of a single part.